W9-BQK-190

THE STRONG COMFORT OF GOD

ERNEST LEE STOFFEL

THE STRONG COMFORT OF GOD

JOHN KNOX PRESS
RICHMOND, VIRGINIA

Library of Congress Catalog Card Number: 58-7774

Printed in the United States of America
5488

To Betty

and

my Mother and Father

contents

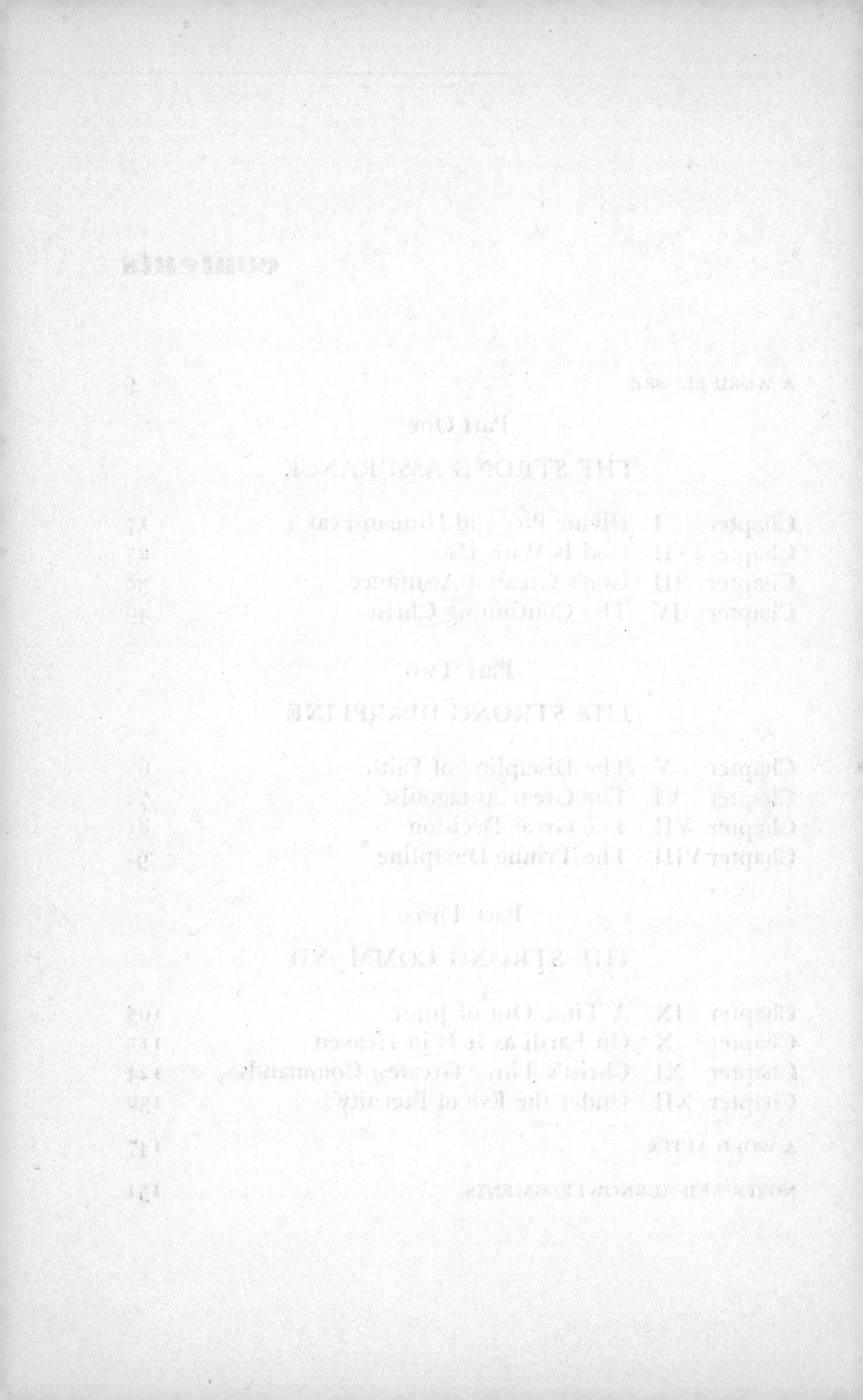

A Word Before

"The secularists have not wrecked divine things; but the secularists have wrecked secular things, if that is any comfort to them. The Titans did not scale heaven; but they laid waste the world."

G. K. CHESTERTON[1]

OUR time is sick for want of God. The secularists have indeed succeeded in destroying secular things; and malajustment has not explained away human sin. Neither have we been able to explain all our predicament in terms of environment. We struggle with global problems of race and national pride against the white glare of a bomb. We are not sure whether the unearthly light of a hydrogen bomb (or by now is there another?) heralds a new world, or merely the death of an old one. We have turned to sleek automobiles and color television. But somehow the same old problems of family, business, human relations, and how to get along with our neighbors keep coming up.

We are ignorant. We have come to the day when we need no vivid reminder of this.[2] Our inability to cope with our confusing world is its own indictment of our ignorance. We laugh and say the more we know the less we know. We probably do not mean it—for science marches on, does it not? T. S. Eliot asks two questions:

> "Where is the wisdom we have lost in knowledge?
> Where is the knowledge we have lost in
> information?
> The cycles of Heaven in twenty centuries
> Bring us farther from God and nearer to the Dust."[3]

The latter statement is certainly extreme pessimism; but who would like to put up a hand and answer Eliot's two questions? Let us not be morbid, however. We are ignorant, certainly; but we are not ready to commit suicide.

We are dust. In spite of our posturings, all our attempts to escape the obvious, we are mortal. And we know it in our deeper thoughts. So we make our funerals more pagan in an attempt to escape the obvious—when we could be singing triumphant hymns.

We are sinners. Such Calvinistic nonsense does not sound like nonsense when our world problems are brought down to the level of the individual man sinning against his neighbor. We have created our own judgment in a bomb, and our guilt is thrust upon us. The bombing of a church in the South, a race riot in the northern United States or South Africa, are of the same parcel with a corrupt government official who uses his position to increase his wealth—and with my failure to get along with my neighbor.

We are afraid. Fears and uncertainties are constant and unpaying guests. They came to dinner long ago, and they are still occupying the spare bedroom. Our fears are almost too numerous to catalogue. We are afraid we will not be adequate for our job or our children. We are fearful of sickness and old age and death. When Pestilence and Fear met in the old legend, Fear rightly boasted that he had destroyed more than Pestilence. Probably there is not one who reads this page at whose heart some anxiety does not tug.

Some would say that we need Divine Judgment today—with a liberal sprinkling of fire and brimstone. Certainly we do not need to forget the fact of judgment and that scales must balance in the universe. It will not do, however, to paint the face of God in wrathful hues, with His eyes flashing judgment. If that is the only God, then let the rocks fall on us.

On the other hand, we do not need a sentimental God. We have scattered too much sentiment about His throne already. A sentimental God is dismissed casually, and too many remain standing when He passes by, instead of bowing their faces to the dust. (Here we could inveigh at length about the "secular" age. When has there been any other?) Yet we do need the assurance of a God who loves us, whose face is turned toward us in mercy as well as judgment. We need a God who is not looking for someone to prostrate himself before Him so much as for someone to turn up a trusting face and lift a trusting hand.

For there are indeed times when our pillows become stones, as was Jacob's pillow at Bethel. Perhaps it is the pillow of remorse, when we are trying to run away from ourselves—only to find that the shadow of what we have been and are is cast before us. Perhaps it is the pillow of grief, an unresolved suspicion that life has played a cruel trick on us and things are not coming out as they should. So our rest becomes a stone.

Perhaps we simply find ourselves a wanderer in life's perplexities and the bewildering rushing events of an age going too fast to catch up with itself. We have more creature comforts, but send more of our creatures to mental institutions, and kill by daily relentless pressure. The tranquilizer only puts off the day when we must face whatever made us take the pill in the first place. For many this age has made their rest a stone.

There must be a God at Bethel. There must be a ladder set up from earth to heaven where a man may meet that God. There must be a God who deeply pities—a God who holds the issues of life in His hands. He must be a God of blessed presence, and not in the remote unreaches of the skies. At the lonely place of the stone—our times—we must meet that God. "Man," says Karl Barth, "does not cry for solutions but for salvation; not for something human, but for God, for God as his Saviour from *humanity*."[4]

This book will say that there is such a God, and that to find Him is to find strong comfort. It was born in the pastorate where the author has the daily responsibility of people. It was born in the pulpit where he has the responsibility of proclaiming the assurances, teaching the disciplines, and declaring the commands of the Christian Faith.

Moreover, this book was born in the conviction that *the layman must have a theology* if he is to live in this day. (We ought not to be afraid of using the word.) And this theology must first be *Biblical*. This theology ought to be presented in uncomplicated and non-technical terms, of course; but by all means it ought to be closely related to the Bible. (For example, the word "discipline" is used many times in this book. It is not so much defined as it is described in Biblical terms. Percy Ainsworth once said that he would not define love because he wanted it understood. Some things are better understood without precise definition.) This book will also have accomplished some purpose if it should stimulate an interest in reading the Bible itself.

This theology must be *well-rounded*. The author as a pastor finds himself deeply concerned along with many others about the easy, self-centered, "peace of mind" school of thinking. The proponents of this emphasis have done us a service in bringing this facet of Christianity to the fore again. But they have gone too far. The layman is receiving a one-sided picture of Christian theology. He is being taught its assurances without hearing of its disciplines or its commands.

So a word of caution at the outset: The God whom this book attempts to present does not give peace without discipline. He will not let us hear His assurances without also hearing His commands. There are no facile formulas for material success or an easy peace of mind in this book. This God gives a gift, but that gift is in a gauntlet. He is a God of blessed assurance and His peace passes all understanding. But banners wave over Him. He calls into a Kingdom that is at war. We must lose ourselves before we find ourselves. We have to take up a cross before we are ready to receive a crown. The Christian Faith has its strong assurance, but also its strong discipline and its strong command. This is the strong comfort of God.

. . . .

The author must again express his appreciation to the officers and congregation of the First Presbyterian Church of Charlotte, North Carolina, for time to prepare the manuscript. Their encouraging interest has been a constant inspiration.

First Presbyterian Church
Charlotte, North Carolina

"As a father pities his children,
so the Lord pities those who fear him.
For he knows our frame;
he remembers that we are dust."

Psalm 103:13-14

PART ONE

THE STRONG ASSURANCE

" 'Tis the weakness in strength, that I cry for!
my flesh, that I seek
In the Godhead!"

ROBERT BROWNING, *"Saul"*

CHAPTER I

Divine Pity and Human Fear

"When I am with God
I look deep down and high up,
And all is changed.
. . . .
My fever is gone
In the great quiet of God.
My troubles are but pebbles on the road,
My joys are like the everlasting hills."

WALTER RAUSCHENBUSCH[1]

THE great search for security and peace of mind stems from fear. Most people are afraid of something most of the time. "Whom shall I fear?" asks the psalmist.[2] Modern man can answer that question in great detail. Some fear death. Some fear economic reverses. Some fear temptation—fear that they shall give in to that dark thing that tugs at their souls and threatens to pull them down. Some fear an unnamed personal calamity that shall come crashing down upon them, shattering their peace or perhaps bringing more unpeace. And over all personal fears there is a kind of world fear. The world draws closer and all men are neighbors; but they do not trust one another.

The popularity of books that promise peace of mind proclaims this deep need in people's hearts. The desire is natural. Man needs a shrine. He cannot long hide from God without feeling the lack.

Modern man can answer the question, "Whom shall I

fear?" but his tragedy is that he cannot affirm in advance: "The Lord is my light and my salvation."[3] High in the Alps at Lucerne, Switzerland, there is a famous peak known as the Burgenstock. Near the summit there are two magnificent hotels where many come to seek rest. Just off the pathway that leads to the summit there is a little chapel. It is almost hidden by the trees. It bears the quiet peace of eternal things. The chapel is a shrine of peace. But few stop there. Most hurry between the hotel and the summit in confusion of soul. Few stop to find the shrine of peace along the way. So modern man continues to hurry between life and an empty mountaintop, and fails to find his shrine along the way.

"AS A FATHER PITIES"

Our fears and confusions will not be stilled unless we find the shrine of God. The psalmist knew that shrine:

> "As a father pities his children,
> so the Lord pities those who fear him."[4]

We may affirm many things about God; but perhaps the greatest is that He is Divine Pity. There is a divine pity at the heart of God which can only be illustrated by the pity which a father has for his children. And yet this simile falls far short.

"The Lord pities those who fear him . . ." "A man who bows down to nothing," said Dostoevski, "can never bear the burden of himself."[5] We cannot bear the burden of ourselves unless we bow down to One greater. In the morass of our ignorance, the uncertainty of our mortality, in the shame of our sins and the quaking terror of our fears, we are not bowing before blind unreasonable law, nor to a stern taskmaster, nor to a rigid, inexorable judge. We are bowing before One with a father's heart—and that greater than any human father's.

"Fear" is a strong word; and a strong word is needed here.

It means that we must cast ourselves upon God with trust, with sincerity, and acknowledge that He alone is wisdom. He is power. When we fly out of this world, we go to Him. When we sin and are penitent, He will forgive. When we find ourselves immersed in some black fear, "The steadfast love of the Lord is from everlasting to everlasting upon those who fear him."[6]

"THE CONSOLATIONS OF GOD"

God "pities." We cannot imagine the full meaning of the pity of God. The embracing largeness of the countenance of God, when it is turned toward us, is beyond comprehension. "Are the consolations of God too small for you?" Eliphaz asks Job in his misery.[7] The consolations of God are never small.

We have the consolations of a God who *knows*. This is not a small thing. Most of the time we want to know, Does God know how I feel? Does He know what I am bearing? Do I look up to nothing and pray to emptiness? Is He like the ancient gods on Olympus, too absorbed in their own pleasures to be concerned about "blight and famine, plague and earthquake . . . clanging fights and flaming towns, and sinking ships, and praying hands"?[8]

We have the consolation of a God who is *able*. The Bible rings with that consolation. The experience of the ages calls to each succeeding generation: "God is able."

> "The eternal God is your dwelling place,
> and underneath are the everlasting arms."[9]

"In my distress I called upon the Lord . . . From his temple he heard my voice," was the triumphant testimony of the psalmist.[10] Against a flaming background of suffering and persecution, Jude writes a little letter to his fellow Christians and concludes with a shout of triumph: "Now to him who is able to keep you from falling and to present you without blemish before the presence of his glory . . ."[11] Never once in the life of Jesus do we find Him doubting that all things are in the hand of the Father.

Periods of discouragement are inevitable, of course. Doubt and spiritual sterility are not unknown to the Christian. Sometimes he finds himself confused and alarmed by life's complexities. He wonders if there is anyone who hears his prayer. And he will ask with the poet: Is there

> "A breath that fleets beyond this iron world,
> And touches Him that made it?"[12]

The answer is that there is not only a breath that fleets beyond this iron world, but that it touches a heart of divine pity. Twice a day the tides come in and power from another world lifts the ships out to sea. So is the man lifted who trusts the tides of God, the lifting power of the Almighty.

When earth's joys grow dim, as they shall; and earth's glories pass away, as they shall; when there is the inevitable change and decay—then it is time to stand beneath the everlasting pity of another world and pray: "O Thou who changest not, abide with me."[13] This is to know the consolation of the divine pity in the heart of God.

A VEIL AND A ROCK

With all of the consolations of God, however, there is always a *veil of mystery* before His face. The impatient will want to tear aside this veil and know immediately all the answers. This is not possible. There will always be some things which we cannot know. The apostles prayed Jesus, "Show us the Father."[14] Let us have done with questions and know the answers. And Moses prayed in sad discouragement after he had broken the tablets of the Ten Commandments before the golden calf: "Show me thy glory."[15]

We can understand the prayer of Moses, as well as the prayer of the apostles. It was an appeal for the answers to the riddle of life. The prayer of the apostles was the prayer of frightened and confused men. The prayer of Moses was the prayer of a frightened and tired man. At the time Moses prayed this prayer, the heavens had seemed to become brass. A rebellion had broken out in the camp and had to be put down with much bloodshed. The situation was desperate and there were no miracles dropping out of the sky. The enemies of Israel might fall upon them at any moment. So Moses prayed, "Show me thy glory."

God's answer seems abrupt: "You cannot see my face."[16] Abrupt or not, there is a truth here that we creatures need to face. There is ultimate mystery at the heart of the universe. There is a veil drawn over the face of God. We are not given all the answers, nor are we admitted into the high counsels of the Almighty.

"You shall see my back; but my face shall not be seen."[17] There is deep truth here. God "passed by" Moses and he saw only God's "back." We hasten as fast as we can, but we only arrive in time to see where God has been. We break the atom and He has been there. We dig into the earth and discover the geologic ages, and God says: "This I have made aeons ago and passed on." We catch a glimpse of His back when a tyrant falls at Waterloo or Berlin. We observe the marvel of human life and the universe and turn to see the Master Creator only as He is closing the door to move on to another task. God "rested" on the seventh day, but shall we assume that He did not begin another work week?

We climb a hill at Calvary. Surely here we shall learn the answers and see God's glory. But the earth reels and blackness descends, and only in darkness broken by scattered flashes of light can we see the mystery of that day when God the Mighty Creator wrought out our salvation.

But if there is a veil of mystery before God, there is also with Him a *rock of assurance*. This is the meaning of that picture of Moses hidden by God in the cleft of a rock—and more especially this is the meaning of what God had to say to Moses while he was in the cleft of the rock: "I will make all my goodness pass before you, and will proclaim before you my name 'The Lord'; and I will be gracious to whom I will be gracious, and will show mercy on whom I will show mercy."[18] The most important thing God has to say to us in our fears is not so much a mighty affirmation of His power, as it is the assurance that He is *a God of unfettered mercy—a God infinitely concerned.*

This is not merely abstract theological truth. The truth is desperately relevant. Thomas Chalmers of Scotland is said to have been a power in the pulpit but often shy in dealing with people. Once a woman in his congregation met with more than the usual amount of life's sorrows, and within a very short time. Chalmers knew that he must go to see her. Several times he circled the block. Finally, he summoned his courage and burst in the door, and without any preamble said: "Madame, I've come to tell you that God bears no ill-will toward you." Brusque and abrupt, perhaps, but graciously and deeply true.

One of the great philosophers once asked: "Is the universe friendly?" It does not take a philosopher to ask that. Anyone who takes the buffetings of life, who marks the course of human tears, who stands beside a grave, asks in one way or another: Is the universe friendly? Does God care about me? This is really what Moses wanted to know and what we all want to know—am I a plaything of the cosmos, or covered by the hand of a concerned God in the cleft of the rock? "He *knows* our frame; he remembers that we are dust."[19]

> "He hideth my soul in the cleft of the rock,
> That shadows a dry thirsty land,
> He hideth my soul in the depths of His love,
> And covers me there with His hand."[20]

IN THE FACE OF JESUS CHRIST

How do we know there is such a God? The prologue to the Gospel according to John answers: "No one has ever seen

God; the only Son, who is in the bosom of the Father, he has made him known."[21] Paul answers the question with a glad shout and points to "the light of the knowledge of the glory of God in the face of Christ."[22]

We turn to One who knew the Father better than any other. Once He faced a crowd of anxious, troubled people—troubled about what they were going to eat, to drink, to wear, troubled about tomorrow and its problems. If Jesus had spoken only these words, life would have become worth the living and the dying: "Your heavenly Father knows . . ."[23]

Jesus came to die at the hands of a rebel world—but He also came to do more than that. He came to say with His life: "The Father knows. The Father cares. The Father is able." He came to say that there is Another World of unfettered mercy and concern.

Shining through all the records of the life of Jesus is His own joyous faith in the Father. It is true, of course, that we are not given all the details of the life of Jesus; but what we are given reveals One who walked upon this earth with sublime courage. Someone will plead that Jesus was Son of God and therefore immune to all the ills of earth—that He walked above it all, wrapped in the clouds; and that He really had no need for the kind of faith we mortals need. But this is not true to the record of His life. The tears were real that He shed before the tomb of His friend Lazarus. The lashes laid upon His back by the Roman whip were real. The betrayer's kiss stabbed to His heart. The sweat that stood out upon His forehead like great drops of blood when He faced the fact of death was not simulated.

He walked among people with their fretting tempers and their ceaseless anxieties. He heard the cries of children and saw His native land in chains forged by a foreign power. He lived in anxiety's drowning sea and faced the end of life like any man. He was "God of God" as the ancient creed says; yet that creed also added, and the confessional voice of the Church has added all these centuries, that He was also One "Who for us men, and for our salvation, came down from heaven . . . *and was made man.*"[24]

Jesus lived as man, and as man He was neighbor to sorrow and anxiety. He had enemies all His public life. He lived in an occupied country. He must have known concern for feeding His mother and brothers and sisters, and may very well have known that desperate anxiety for a wayward brother or sister. Yet His face was not long and dour. He entered into clean human joys. He loved dinner parties, and whenever there was a wedding in the area, Jesus was invited. Children ran to Him that He might touch them—a sure sign of a happy personality.

His faith in the face of anxiety and trouble is a shining thing. He said, "Do not be anxious about your life, what you shall eat or what you shall drink."[25] But He did not mean that we should be lazy or thoughtless about the necessities of life for ourselves and our families. Most of His adult life Jesus probably labored in a carpenter shop. He meant needless anxiety that comes from a lack of faith in the Father in heaven.

Over the life of Jesus there is written a sublime faith in the Father. He believed life was good in spite of pain. He saw the beauty of the flowers and the loving care God puts upon the common grass "which today is alive and tomorrow is thrown into the oven."[26] He listened to the song of birds and saw that they lived by some beneficent hand without storehouse or barn. He knew the Father, not as one to shrink from, but as one to love.

His eyes would often stray to the strained faces of people. Here was a priest, concerned about his place in the Temple. Here was a publican, never knowing when on a dark night someone would thrust a knife into him. On the edge of the crowd was the strained face of a woman of the streets, wondering if honor was ever possible to her again. Here was a father with a son in his arms and care on his face. These were people—anxious, discouraged, concerned. His gaze would take them all in, and then He would gently say: ". . . your heavenly Father knows."[27]

Jesus taught that the doors of heaven are not closed to our prayers: "Ask, and it will be given you; seek, and you will find; knock, and it will be opened to you."[28] He taught that we pray a heavenly Father who in His love will give "more" than our earthly fathers in their love which is tainted by earth's sin: "If you then, who are evil, know how to give good gifts to your children, how much more will the heavenly Father . . . ?"[29]

Jesus also taught that in the sight of heaven, a human being is of infinite worth: "You are of more value than many sparrows. . . . Of how much more value is a man than a sheep!"[30] The Divine Pity is even upon the sparrow. "You are of more value . . ." God is like a shepherd leaving ninety and nine and looking for the one lost. He is like a poor woman sweeping every nook and cranny until she finds the lost coin. He is the father who waits interminable hours and days in agonizing concern for a prodigal son.

Jesus did teach one fear: "And do not fear those who kill the body but cannot kill the soul; rather fear him who can destroy both soul and body in hell."[31] Certainly Jesus had no fear of those who can kill the body. He met them without fear and heard them out mostly in silence. But His example indicates that the evil one should be met with the sword of the Word of God.

Part of the saving work of Jesus is not only salvation from sin, but salvation from fear. And it is significant that it was as man and not as God that He saved from fear. No legions of angels were invoked. No stones were turned into bread. When we seek to exalt Jesus as God only, then we lose this part of His salvation. He shared the earth with us. His eyes turned upward. "I have loved to hear my Lord spoken of," said Mr. Standfast in *Pilgrim's Progress*. "And wherever I have seen the print of His shoe in the earth, there I have coveted to set my foot too."[32] The print of Christ's shoe is along the common ways of earth where we all must walk. It is before a carpenter's bench, a mother's anxious face, a friend's grave. It is before a cross. But the tread is not of one who walks with heavy heart and head bent, with eyes that see no light. It is the tread of One who walked with joyous faith, and to whom life was one great shout of victory.

Jesus is the Divine Pity. He is that consolation of God come down to earth. In the face of Jesus Christ this "glory" of God comes into focus. In Him something of the veil of mystery is taken away. We are given some answers—indeed, we are given the most important answers. So "Christ can give thee heart," as Christina Rossetti says.

> ". . . Christ can give thee heart Who loveth thee:
> Can set thee in the eternal ecstasy
> Of His great jubilee:
> Can give thee dancing heart and shining face,
> And lips filled full of grace,
> And pleasures as the rivers and the sea."[33]

The secret is to know Him, as God and as Man. In Jesus the consolations of God are large enough and loving enough to embrace the world. In Jesus the Divine Pity was incarnate. Has He indeed been so long time with us, and yet we have not known Him? To see Him is to see the Father. A world desperately seeking peace and assurance pushes past Him on its panting climb to the summit. But to the summit of what? The Divine Pity of Christ sweeps over a world that does not know "the things that make for peace."[34] He has been a long time with us. It is time to look at Him again.

CHAPTER II

God Is With Us

"O that thou wouldst rend the heavens and come down . . ."

"Why then did He not appear by means of other and nobler parts of creation . . . instead of man merely? . . . The Lord came not to make a display, but to heal and teach those who were suffering."[1]

THE Divine Pity has come down and dwelt among us. God has built a bridge from earth to heaven. At one end of the bridge is a manger. Along the way of the bridge is a cross and an open tomb. At the other end are the eternal stars. This is the central truth of Christianity. The divine has visited the human. Heaven has come to earth. God is with us in Jesus Christ.

"CALL HIS NAME IMMANU-EL"

Men have long yearned and looked for this visitation. Outstanding among these men in the Old Testament was the prophet Isaiah. It was he who first used the word "Immanuel" or Immanu-el—"With us God." He told King Ahaz and the people of Israel that their faith should be in the God who was with them in power—that they should not trust in horses and chariots or foreign alliances alone to save them.[2] This is the central meaning in Isaiah 7:14. Again and again Isaiah declared that God was with them and they should put their trust in Him.

But Isaiah looked for more. He looked for Immanuel to

be clothed with form and flesh and to visit His people. This is the basic message of Isaiah 9:2–6.

"The people who walked in darkness
have seen a great light . . .

. . . .

For to us a child is born . . ."[3]

No earthly king of Israel or Judah was ever able to fulfill the lofty requirements of Isaiah's "child"-king:

"Wonderful Counselor, Mighty God,
Everlasting Father, Prince of Peace."[4]

This King would possess these attributes of divinity—but most important of all, He would be of earth—"for to us a child is born." He would be flesh of our flesh and bone of our bone. He would be born "to us." He would be truly "God with us." Man will not be satisfied until God walks with him again in the garden.[5] Man will not be redeemed until God walks with him again in the garden.

The New Testament writers, notably Matthew, with the life of Jesus before them could come to only one conclusion.[6] This was "Immanu-el." Jesus was Immanuel—God with us. Jesus was God come down to earth to be with us in redeeming power. Jesus was the only one who ever fulfilled the lofty requirements of Isaiah's "child"-king. He walked the earth with attributes of deity, but He was also bone of our bone and flesh of our flesh. In Him God walked with us again in the garden of earth.

" 'I cannot reach you, God,' I cried,
And stretched my arms up toward the blue.
He smiled, and took me by the hand
And said, 'Then I'll reach down to you.' "[7]

THE GRACE OF OUR LORD JESUS CHRIST

The Christian Faith calls this coming of God to be with us "grace." The Old Testament did picture God as gracious, but the New Testament gave form and substance to the idea when it added: "the grace of our Lord Jesus Christ." "For you know the grace of our Lord Jesus Christ," said Paul, "that though he was rich, yet for your sake he became poor, so that by his poverty you might become rich."[8]

Jesus was the grace of God "with us." Let us use another word: Jesus was the grace of God *incarnate.* Grace spoke from His lips and was in His healing hand. In all of the Gospels, the word "grace" is not used more than two or three times. The Gospel writers were simply looking at the face of Jesus Christ. They did not have to use the word, for grace was walking among them. They observed His gracious acts and listened to His gracious words: "Come to me, all who labor and are heavy-laden, and I will give you rest."[9] And they believed that this was what their fathers had called the loving-kindness of God.

"He was rich, yet for your sake he became poor."[10] The very words cry out for men to turn and look in amazement. Certainly sentiment has played too long on this theme and has greatly overdone it. Yet a great truth remains—the sacrifice of Deity entering history and humanity. Rich is a poor human word to describe the glory of heaven. "He had come from God,"[11] said John simply, and then closed the door. The light streaming out was too much for mortal eyes.

Why should God come to earth and suffer? "Yet for your sake," replies Paul, and we cannot find another reason. Here is love without measure—amazing truth that no other religion in the world knows. The heart of the Creator is actually constrained by love for His creatures, to the point where He will come to earth and suffer. This, too, He did in spite of the fact that they have looked up into His face and said, "No!"

Certainly we did not call Him down; nor have we gone to Him. It is man's nature to hide from the Creator, since the days of Eden. A few cloistered hearts through the ages have yearned to see some earnest of His love, but the multitudes have gone on getting and spending, and the thought of the Creator lingers only a little in their hearts.

God took the initiative. "He became poor." Although we

cannot look into the heavenly, the earthly life of the Son of God is known from humble birth until tragic death. It can best be described in three words: "He became poor." The sacrifice of Jesus was not just a legalistic blood sacrifice. It was far more than that. It was God impoverishing Himself for our sake.

"THE WORD BECAME FLESH"

"And the Word became flesh and dwelt among us."[12] The Divine Pity dwelt among us. God is with us. God became man. We are immediately in the presence of something that goes far beyond our ken. The simplicity of the Christmas story can be deceiving—the poor couple, the child born in a manger, the shepherds, angels, and Wise Men. Many have turned away with a reverent smile and concluded that this story is only for children. Yet the one great philosophical passage in the New Testament, the one using the loftiest language and the very deepest thought, is the prologue of the Gospel according to John which speaks of the birth of Jesus Christ. When we read it, we are face to face with eternal things.

"The Word"—the very expression of God Himself, which was in the beginning with God and was God and by whom all things were made—"became flesh." A number of very large exclamation points should be written after that. Dorothy L. Sayers declares that she stares in bewilderment at people who assure her Christianity leaves them cold, as being a dull affair that bores them.

The *Word* became *flesh*. Here are two words as far apart as they could possibly be. Logos (Word) in Greek thinking meant all that man can know of God. Sarx (flesh) in Greek thought meant something essentially evil. The Christian Faith dares to bring these two things together. By taking flesh, God brought these two things together!

Something of the idea that flesh is evil is still with us. It is common to speak in the same breath of "the world, the flesh, and the devil." But when we realize what Christianity is teaching about Jesus Christ we are thrown back upon the question: If flesh were essentially evil, how could the Son of God clothe Himself in it? The answer must be that *flesh is not in itself evil*—only those who inhabit flesh.

Moreover, the Word became flesh, and this is our *dignity*. Our flesh is not a mantle of iniquity. We possess a great dignity, for the robes of earth have also draped the Son of God. From this arises the stubborn insistence of Christians that there is a dignity to each individual that will not permit any system of tyranny to immerse people in the mass. Flesh has been honored and dignified with the life of God. The yearning of the human spirit to rise above the life of the animal has been honored.

The Word became flesh, God is with us, and *prayer is a reality*. Is there a God to whom it is any use to pray for forgiveness, for help, for redress of the world's wrongs? If He has gone off somewhere to hang a bright star, my hands are lifted to emptiness. If He is away in another galaxy, busy with a million worlds other than mine, then what need for rededicating life to the good? But we pray to an intimate Friend.

God has entered the world and *we are not alone*. In our deeper thoughts we know that there is no redemption from earth. If man is alone upon the earth, then he is terribly alone indeed. We are fragile, for all our gadgets; we are forever mocked by our mortality. We may beat vainly upon the doors of the sky only to discover that the universe is flying away from us. The stars we see are ghosts, and the real stars, if they are still there, are hundreds of billions of miles away. So then the yearning question: Is God with us, or is He only some "dreaming dark dumb Thing who turns the handle of this idle show"?[13] But the "Word became flesh and dwelt among us." "And dwelt among us"—woven into the life of the Son of God were the threads of a manger cradle, the cruelty of a dictator, a home in Nazareth, a carpenter shop, a wedding, crowds, pain, evil, joy, loyalty, and treachery. Life's joys and sorrows are not unknown to the Eternal. Life is a pilgrimage with a Friend.

God is with us, and *life is an adventure*. Certainly there is no point in committing ourselves in faith to a God who has coldly turned His back, or who at best is neutral. If God be not with us, then we are pathetic Don Quixotes tilting at windmills. We had better take off our foolish knight's armor and bend our eyes to the clay from whence we came. But if God is with us, then life can be an adventure of venturing faith. We shall cry to the years that we are ready for them. We shall walk through our days with a strong Companion. Life's battles are not met alone but with Him who hallows and preserves life—with Him who honored life with His Life.

The Word became flesh—and *the earth is not our final sphere*. He has descended that we may ascend. God built a bridge from a star to a manger. Along that bridge we may have commerce with the Eternal and cross over to glory. Write these haunting lines from G. K. Chesterton over the manger of Bethlehem:

> "To an open house in the evening
> Home shall men come,
> To an older place than Eden
> And a taller town than Rome:
> To the end of the way of the wandering star,
> To the things that cannot be and that are,
> To the place where God was homeless
> And all men are at home."[14]

"The Word became flesh." God was homeless that all men might be at home.

"HE SAW THE MULTITUDES"

But perhaps the greatest truth of all in the Incarnation is that *God looked at the world through the eyes of Jesus Christ.*

He looked at men—eye to eye; He knew the raucous bargaining of the market, the subtle maneuverings of the politician, the daily struggle of men for bread. "But when he saw the multitudes, he was moved with compassion on them, because they fainted, and were scattered abroad, as sheep having no shepherd."[15] One day the men closest to Jesus Christ saw a sight they would never forget. Jesus was looking at people and there were tears in His eyes. God was looking at people and there were tears in His eyes.

Along the edges of the crowd were death and disease, blindness and dumbness, and the troubled conscience that needed desperately a word of forgiveness. God's eyes saw the frayed strands of earth's tapestry as well as its golden threads. Here was a prodigal hurrying on his way to the big city, sure that soon now he would begin to live. Here was a girl toying with the idea of flinging herself into the gaiety of the world regardless of the consequences. Here was a merchant, hard pressed by the taxes of Rome and at the same time under pressure to show a profit. A farmer anxiously scanned the skies for rain. God's eyes saw those burdened by sleepless nights and brooding fears, and the sheer wear and tear of life. Napoleon looked at people and saw cannon fodder. But Jesus Christ looked at people and saw frightened sheep.

God through Christ saw the multitudes—not as a crowd, pressing on Him, demanding His time, taking away His energies, plucking at His sleeve with this and that request—but as people, *as individuals*. The woman who touched His robe was a person. The important ruler of the synagogue was a grief-stricken father. The two blind men trying to lead one another along were to others either objects of amusement or a nuisance, but to Jesus they were two men. The dumb man had already been dismissed by everyone: "He has a devil."[16] But Jesus saw a man in front of Him, perhaps a man stricken by some deep melancholia, induced by who knows what dark shadow that had fallen across his life. And now he had shut himself up in his own soul, closed and barred the doors and spoken to no man. Jesus saw him as a man with his face lined with indescribable sorrow.

"He saw the multitudes"—He saw and He *knew*. His eyes did not stray carelessly over the crowd. Behind the pretense He saw the pathos. Behind the sneer He saw the sin. "He knew what was in man," said one of the Gospel writers.[17] Those clear eyes would see the weakness, that which needed to go. The pretense would be singled out. The sin would be revealed. For this reason, some went away from Him with flushed and angry faces.

But those who lingered found that He put His finger upon the potentialities of greatness and of goodness within them. He showed people the stars in their lives, as Tennyson says. Some went away with a quiet peace in their hearts. The angry waves of anxiety and the high winds of fear were stilled. "He was moved with compassion"—and the word is too weak to bear the full meaning. It literally means "pain of love," but even that is not enough to describe the outgoing healing grace of Jesus Christ. He walked among men and mingled His tears with their own, and in that mingling men found healing and peace.

> "I looked for Christ in the hidden skies,
> A flaming vision to blind my eyes—
> While Christ walked by with stumbling feet
> Along with the men of Madison Street."[18]

And when men touched Him who was Compassion Incarnate, *they were delivered*. It was more than just a deliverance of the body. Jesus healed comparatively few actually. His followers in His name have healed far more through the ministry of Christian hospitals, doctors, and nurses. Indeed, He often sternly charged those who were healed not to publish the fact, for He did not wish to be regarded only as miracle worker.

Jesus desired to give a greater deliverance. For what good

are life and health if you do not know what to do with them? What good is life restored if it have no purpose? What good is sight if you cannot really see your neighbor? What good is speech, unless it be the speech of love and understanding? Jesus gave people the ability to see, not just chattels and things, but trees and color and beauty, love, gratitude, and faith, goodness and charity. He taught them to live a gallant life of faith that one day rides in triumph into the Holy City. He opened the mouths of the dumb that they might speak with their neighbors, not as churls, but with words of kindness and understanding. Jesus delivered to life eternal, not just to physical life alone. He would give deliverance that men would know how to live for eternity now. "I am come," He said, "that they might have life, and that they might have it more abundantly."[19]

God through Jesus looks at our lives and gently reminds us that they are more than just meat, drink, and raiment.[20] Life is more than living twenty-four hours a day. Life is more than seeing. God sees us, knows us, and would deliver us to a life of peace and power. This is the God who is "with us." This is why Christmas is the most joyous festival of the human spirit. We celebrate God's day of birth among us because our lives are now shared by God. It is our daily comfort that God has looked at the world and us through the eyes of Jesus Christ. We call Him "Lord," and He is indeed the Master of souls. We call Him "Physician," and certainly He is the Healer of souls. But best of all, in life's throng and press we call Him "Friend."

"HE CAME TO HIS OWN"

We must now follow Immanuel to one more place. God came to be with us. The Word became flesh. The Divine Pity entered the world—but to what end? The prologue of the Gospel according to John answers in the most tragic sentence in the Bible, indeed in all literature: "He came to his own home, and his own people received him not."[21] Man is not capable of writing sadder words. For what is sadder than to come to one's own and not be received? This is the tragedy of God.

When we trace the steps of God among us, we follow them finally to a cross. Strange that God would come to be with us and not be crowned and enthroned. This is the tragedy of man—that he was not capable of receiving God when God was with him. "His own people received him not." The cross stands as a stark reminder of this fact.

Yet the cross is not so much a symbol of our condemnation as it is a symbol of our glory. Christians sing, "In the cross of Christ I glory"; and we do not glory in that which condemns us. Paul gives us the answer: "But God shows his love for us in that while we were yet sinners Christ died for us." . . . "While we were yet helpless, at the right time Christ died for the ungodly."[22] *The cross is our glory because God came knowing what we are.* We were "sinners." We were "helpless." Yet He came.

Moreover, the New Testament even makes bold to suggest that *this coming was not a thing of casual moment with God.* It was "destined before the foundation of the world."[23] And here we stand before as great a mystery as the Word becoming flesh: "You know," suggests the first letter of Peter, "that you were ransomed . . . not with perishable things such as silver or gold, but with the precious blood of Christ, like that of a lamb without blemish or spot. He was destined before the foundation of the world . . ."[24] Here our minds reach a stopping place before the infinite mind of God. The cross assumes eternal proportions.

"He came to his own . . ." The simple words have a comfort all their own. He came knowing what we are. Indeed, "He was destined before the foundation of the world." This is our blessed hope. He did come—and there is something in us that is part of God and eternity. For He did not come to a people of foreign speech. He came to His own, although He was to be cruelly used and rejected. Nothing could keep

Him from coming. The Divine Pity has rent the heavens and come down, and we have seen our "flesh . . . in the Godhead."[25]

"God is with us . . . Unto us a child is born . . . The Word became flesh . . . He saw the multitudes and had compassion . . . He came to his own." The words ring with strong assurance. They must be written down, not with a period but with a doxology.

CHAPTER III

God's Greatest Assurance

> "Thou wert with me, but I was not with Thee. Things held me far from Thee . . . Thou calledst and shoutedst and didst pierce my deafness . . . And now my whole life is in nothing but in Thine exceeding great mercy."
>
> AUGUSTINE[1]

IF God came down to us in Christ, then surely He has something of paramount importance to say to us. He came to assure us that He is a God infinitely concerned for us. That concern is written upon the face and actions of Jesus Christ. The Divine Pity walked among us in Jesus. Our flesh assumed a new dignity. Prayer became not shouting to the sky, but conversation with a Friend. Life became an adventure with a strong Companion. And we dare look up and believe that this earth is not our sphere.

But all this is not enough. We should not be churls, of course, and fling these mercies back in God's face. Yet there is another need; and to this need God speaks His greatest word—the assurance of forgiveness.

Now let us not debate sin, or be labeled like the preacher who was merely "agin it." One Old Testament word for sin is transgression of a known law. There is another Old Testament word for sin which is the picture of something crooked or distorted. The New Testament word for sin is the most tragic. It is the picture of a man shooting at a target and missing the mark. Here we must look deep—not morbidly but realistically. Who has not transgressed? Can we point to everything in our lives as absolutely straight? And who has not missed the mark—failed to live up to the best or the purest? Failure is not a popular word today. But in our honest moments, we know we have "failed."

"AGAINST THEE ONLY HAVE I SINNED"

But whom or what have we failed? Whose Law has been transgressed? Where is that "straightness" beside which our distortion is plainly seen?

The psalmist prays:

> "Wash me thoroughly from my iniquity,
> and cleanse me from my sin!
> For I know my transgressions,
> and my sin is ever before me.
> *Against thee,* thee only, have I sinned . . ."[2]

And Isaiah cries in agony: "Woe is me! For I am lost; for I am a man of unclean lips . . . *for my eyes have seen the King,* the Lord of hosts!"[3] Both are looking at their own wrongdoing, of course; but more than that they are looking at God. What they see in God drives them to their knees. The psalmist acknowledges that his wrongdoing on earth is first a transgression against the God in heaven. Isaiah sees his sin, after he has seen the King sitting upon an everlasting throne.

What kind of God do the people in the Bible see? They certainly are not looking at an amoral God who does not care for what is right and what is wrong. On the contrary, they see a God whose laws are righteous and have been transgressed. He is the universal "straightness" beside which all things look distorted or crooked. But above all else, they see a "holy" God. The word "holy" in Hebrew means "separate." And when applied to God it means One who is removed from sinful man by His very purity. Hence when Isaiah heard the angelic choirs cry, "Holy, holy, holy is the Lord of hosts,"[4] then he saw himself as unclean. Isaiah saw also a great gap between himself and God. This holy God cannot look at iniquity. Because of what He is, He is holy—separated from it.

"THE HOLY ONE IN YOUR MIDST"

A vision of this holy, separated God only drives to despair. It is not comfortable, to say the least, to think of a holy God sitting upon the throne of the universe—a God whose wrath waxes hot against the sinfulness of man. Yet the Bible does see such a God, and men fall on their faces before Him. And in our day, we could do with more falling upon faces before Him also. For the wrath of God is still a terrible reality, and secular man does not know it.

Nevertheless, a separated God of wrath only drives men to the dust, but does not lift them up. Hence the agony of the men in the Old Testament. Who or what would bridge the gap between sinful man and holy God?

Isaiah remained on his face until a remarkable thing happened. An angel took a coal from the high altar of God and laid it upon Isaiah's lips, and pronounced the words of absolution: "Behold, this has touched your lips; your guilt is taken away, and your sin forgiven."[5] The psalmist dared to believe:

> "The sacrifice acceptable to God is a broken spirit;
> a broken and contrite heart, O God, thou wilt not despise."[6]

And the prophet Hosea dares to declare this of a holy God:

> "For I am God and not man,
> *the Holy One in your midst,*
> and I will not come to destroy."[7]

What else were these men seeing in the nature of God besides His wrath and holiness? They were seeing a God who would forgive. They were seeing a God of love and infinite mercy *who would Himself bridge the gap between man's sin and His own holiness.* He was the Holy One in their midst. Yet they were not destroyed, but redeemed!

Indeed, Hosea draws one of the boldest and most hopeful pictures of God in the Bible. Hosea pictures God as a husband betrayed by his bride, a loving husband who will yet take back his wayward wife. God through Hosea speaks to a wayward Israel: "And I will betroth you to me forever; I will betroth you to me in righteousness and in justice, in steadfast love, and in mercy."[8] And, in another figure of speech, Hosea pictures God as a wronged father who will not cut off his prodigal son. Here is some of the greatest insight into the nature of God in the Old Testament:

> "When Israel was a child, I loved him,
>
> . . . .
>
> Yet it was I who taught Ephraim to walk,
> I took them up in my arms;
>
> . . . .
>
> My people are bent on turning away from me;
>
> . . . .
>
> How can I give you up, O Ephraim!"[9]

In other words, there is something else in the heart of God besides wrath and judgment—something which we can only dimly appreciate. For, as Hosea says also, He is "God and not man."[10] For want of a better phrase, we must call it simply "the love of God." It is this indefinable something in the nature of God that bridges the gap between Himself and sinful man:

> "How can I give you up, O Ephraim!
>
> . . . .
>
> My heart recoils within me,
> my compassion grows warm and tender."[11]

"I WILL ARISE AND GO TO MY FATHER"

Hosea's picture of a heartbroken Father in heaven is fully drawn in Jesus' incomparable parable of the prodigal son.[12] Hosea's poignant phrases are echoed again in the parable; and our attention is finally brought not so much to the penitent prodigal as to the waiting father.

There is something of the prodigal in all of us. The prodigal can be, of course, a wastrel bent on wasting all his substance in riotous living. But he need not necessarily be so gross as this. For the prodigal is first a self-centered man: "Give me the portion of goods that falleth to me."[13] The prodigal forgets that no man's life belongs exclusively to him alone but to the Father who gave it. And to forget this in any way is to become a prodigal in life and prodigal with life. Also, the prodigal never intends to become a failure, or to sacrifice his honor and purity. Neither does anyone—at first. With tragic simplicity, Jesus describes the prodigal's descent into hell: "The younger son gathered all he had and took his journey into a far country, and there he squandered his property in loose living."[14]

And who has not been in the "far country" of the prodigal? The far country can be the country of the wastrel and the man who gives himself grossly to the demands of the flesh and the world. But again, it need not be so. For the far country reduced to simple terms is the country far from home. It is a descent from the best, a refusal of the highest. The far country is a country without prayer, without Bible; where no man says "I believe" and every man says "I doubt." The creed of that country is to believe what one can see and to live for what one can get. It is a place where fame is important, where things are absolutely necessary; where success is put above character, and reputation is put above inner goodness. When a man is in the far country he feels that he has arrived and has found his place in the world. Actually, he has not arrived anywhere and the world has found its place in him. The far country can be very near.

In the far country, eventually a "mighty famine" always arises. It can be a famine in which a man has wasted his honor and his substance and finds himself left with nothing. But it can also be a famine in which a man has done everything and made everything and still finds a famine in his soul. In any event, it always remains profoundly true that a man must "come to himself." The prodigal in Jesus' parable came to himself in pain, hunger, shame, and loneliness: "I will arise and go to my father, and I will say to him, 'Father, I have sinned against heaven and before you; I am no longer worthy to be called your son . . .' "[15]

But here we must ask a question: Upon what grounds can we assume that there is any use to arise and go to our Father? What good does it do for a man to say, "I will go home," if there is no one at home waiting to love and receive him? Even when we come to a realization of our sin, a still more terrible question presents itself: Is there Anyone who will forgive? We are again with Isaiah on his face in the Temple. And here the New Testament links with the Old in even greater reassurance: "But when he was yet a great way off, his father saw him, and had compassion."[16] The waiting father in the parable is a picture of God; and his vigil is the vigil of Heaven over a prodigal world. The gap is again bridged by God: "How can I give you up, O Ephraim!"[17] To look deeply at our sin is to look fully at the Father in heaven who is waiting to forgive when we "come to ourselves."

"THE HOUND OF HEAVEN"

Sometimes we arise and go to our Father, but more often than not it is the Father who comes looking for us. The harsh word "condemn" is seldom if ever on the lips of Jesus. He prefers that pathetic and desperate word "lost." It is a word with tears in it. There is nothing more apt to wring sympathy from the hardest-hearted man than a lost child. Jesus said that in the eyes of God there is nothing more pathetic than a lost man.

It may come as a shock to some that Heaven looks upon us as lost sheep or coins or sons in need of being found again.[18] Surely we know where we are and where we are going? But how far from Eden or the story of Cain and Abel have we really come? The story of Cain is re-enacted in Lidice (or have we forgotten?)—and in Budapest, to the accompaniment of tanks instead of rocks. Pushing back to that ultimate story, the story of Eden where all of our history is found in miniature, we are confronted with Man (the word "Adam" means Man) and with ourselves. We may use atomic bombs instead of stone axes, but our souls are the same—capable of being lost or found, dwelling in the sight of God's face or being thrust out with His disfavor upon us.

This "lostness" we know in our humbler moments. But when this "lostness," this sense of not being right with our Maker, confronts us with its dark shadow, there are varying reactions. Some try to escape into a world of feverish amusement. Some intellectually try to write God off—only to meet His eye in a test tube or in a flying star, or in some law written into the universe which cannot be explained without a Lawmaker. The Pharisees and their counterparts in every age have said: "We will seek to placate God by our righteousness. It may be that by what we do or what we are we shall find favor in His sight. We will keep the Law and we will add more to it. Through it we will find our salvation." But their self-righteousness only cankers into a burdensome thing which no man can keep or into an unlovely thing which no man will have.

The publicans and sinners (and prodigals) in every age have despaired of this. They have nothing to offer God but a tattered conscience. If God were waiting to be placated by their lives, then they know they have no hope. They are lost and condemned, and the best for which they can hope is to go unnoticed by Heaven.

Hence at this point there is another picture of God. God is holy—separated from sin by His holiness. God is love and bridges the gap between man's sin and His holiness. But God does not continue to sit in remote holiness upon His throne. He goes out into the night like a shepherd seeking one lost sheep: "Does he not leave the ninety-nine in the wilderness, and go after the one which is lost, until he finds it?"[19] He is like a poor woman who sweeps the house until she finds the lost coin: "Does she not light a lamp . . . and seek diligently until she finds it?"[20] While the prodigal is a great way off, God runs to meet him: "But while he was yet at a distance, his father saw him and had compassion . . ."[21]

God seeks—*in spite of how little we are.* The skeptic will sneer that the God of the universe might bother to look for a lost planet that has broken loose from its sun, but He would not bother with a lost man. Indeed, why would God bother even with this insignificant planet? But that sneer cannot push by the parable of the lost sheep. Moreover, the philosophy that makes a man a mere cog in a wheel, a number, a statistic, or even a color, cannot stand in the same place with the parable of the prodigal son.

God seeks us—*in spite of what we are.* We can understand the search for a great and good man like Livingstone, but would anyone come looking for us, considering what we know about ourselves? Does God care about a prodigal or one human coin of a soul, when there are ninety and nine gathered in? Surely "love is patient and kind" was written not only of the way we ought to be, but of the way God is.[22]

God seeks us—but let us not forget, *not without great cost to Himself.* The shepherd braved the wilderness. The woman swept diligently and tearfully. The father waited interminable hours in an agony of suspense, and gave of his forgiveness without stint. And these are but pictures that fall far short of the truth they are teaching.

So we return to "the Word became flesh" and remember that "He was rich, yet for your sake he became poor."[23] At Bethlehem's cradle, God was seeking us. What did it cost for Deity to take the pains of humanity? "How silently, how silently the wondrous Gift is given," said Phillips Brooks in his beloved hymn. But at what tremendous cosmic cost! God was seeking us upon a cross. For when God would seek His world with His most searching call, it was not in the courts of the world or high upon its mountaintops, but upon a cross. The message of the cross to humanity is: "Someone was here looking for you. He left a message that He would call again—and again—and again."

A cross was reared on Calvary. It has long since crumbled away; but there is a cross forever planted in heaven. It is God's pain of love looking far down the centuries to those who are "afar off." The cross is God's waiting and suffering for those whom He loves.

In Semitic countries there was once a beautiful custom called the sacrifice of the threshold. If a son, through rebellion or legitimately, left home and returned, there was always a sacrifice made on the threshold to celebrate his return. So the cross is God's sacrifice on the threshold. It is God's pledge of forgiveness and the bridging of an awful gap. Yet, too, it is God going out into the night of earth.

"But none of the ransomed ever knew
How deep were the waters crossed;
Nor how dark was the night that the Lord
passed through
Ere He found His sheep that was lost.
Out in the desert He heard its cry—
Sick and helpless, and ready to die.

" 'Lord, whence are those blood drops all the way
That mark out the mountain's track?'
'They were shed for one that had gone astray
Ere the shepherd could bring him back.'
'Lord, whence are Thy hands so rent and torn?
'They're pierced tonight by many a thorn.' "[24]

Of course there is Shaw's sneer: "Forgiveness is a beggar's refuge. A man must pay his debts."[25] Aye, but in what coin?

With what coin shall a man pay the debts of his soul? The publican in the parable would gladly have paid every cent he had, if it would have shriven his soul.[26] We are brought to a terrible impasse, unless there is a God who will forgive our sins. We may proclaim an all-powerful God and offer all-convincing and undeniable proofs; but men will fling that gospel back in our faces unless we can demonstrate that that all-powerful God will also visit us in our extremity.

God has visited us in Jesus Christ. The greatest thing God had to say to us through Christ is that our sins can be forgiven. God is far more interested in seeking and reclaiming a lost humanity than in consigning a lost humanity to hell. He cannot give up Ephraim. He has dispatched His "angel" from the high altar and laid that "coal" upon the lips of man—even His Son. Heaven has forgotten its dignity and gone out into the night seeking the lost.

Francis Thompson has called Him the "Hound of Heaven." And Francis Thompson's life is an illustration of his poem. He was born to be a poet, but was cut off by a misunderstanding father. In London he barely kept alive selling matches and calling cabs at theater doors. Finally he took to laudanum to deaden his misery. One day he scribbled a few verses on some dirty scraps of paper and slipped them through the door of the journal *The Merry England.* The editor, Mr. Wilfred Meynell, found them and recognized their worth. Immediately he began a search for the author. When he found Thompson, he was able to reclaim him from the gutter; and Francis Thompson spent the rest of his life writing and in honor. His greatest poem, "The Hound of Heaven," is his own account of the God who would never let him go and who finally found him:

"I fled Him, down the nights and down the days;
I fled Him down the arches of the years;
I fled Him down the labyrinthine ways
Of my own mind . . ."

One day he stopped running and Christ spoke to him:

> " 'Whom wilt thou find to love ignoble thee
> Save Me, save only Me?' "

He closes his poem with this beautiful suggestion:

> "Halts by me that footfall:
> Is my gloom, after all,
> Shade of His hand, outstretched caressingly?
> 'Ah, fondest, blindest, weakest,
> I am He Whom thou seekest!
> Thou dravest love from thee, who dravest Me.' "[27]

"But when he was yet a great way off"—and who of us has not been at some time a great way off?—"his father saw him, and had compassion."[28]

CHAPTER IV

The Continuing Christ

"That one Face, far from vanish, rather grows,
Or decomposes but to recompose,
Become my universe that feels and knows!"

ROBERT BROWNING[1]

THE Christian Faith declares that God has come to earth in Jesus Christ. He was the "grace" of God in visible action and form. His coming was mystery, but what He said and did was plain for all to see. His miracles were like flags that fly over a general's tent to indicate that the commander is on the field. His teachings made men hear commands, and feel forever dissatisfied with the booths of the world. His coming was God's great assurance that we are not alone. But above all else, He assured us of a loving Father in heaven, and died that we might be forgiven.

Yet He was used most cruelly by cruel men—or at best by thoughtless men—and was put to death. He was enthroned upon a cross. From God's side of things it was an act of love; but from our side it was the indelible mark of our sin. Here are some of the most final words ever written: "And . . . rolled a stone against the door of the tomb."[2] Without embellishment they state an accomplished fact. For when the piercing tragedy of Calvary was over and the crosses no longer hung against the sky and stabbed the earth with shame, many people would have put a period and called the matter finished.

THE DAY AFTER CALVARY

The day after Calvary the crowd went home to their own thoughts as crowds must. Caiaphas and Annas were well satisfied. The money-changers could go back to the Temple and ply their trade. Perhaps Pilate spent some uneasy hours. Did Barabbas carouse all night in some local tavern to celebrate his release? One dark figure hung silently between heaven and earth; better for that man if he had not been born.

The apostles would long remember that they forsook and fled. As Browning has it: It was "a torchlight and a noise, the sudden Roman faces, violent hands"—and they all forsook Him and fled.[3] Now their cause was lost—nailed to a cross and irrevocably sealed with death's finality on the other side of a stone.

One by one they came back to the place of the last supper. The words of Jesus were still hanging in the air, like a beautiful melody that is gone forever. Like many another desperate soul they must have thought that they could not bear it. They could not pray, and the words were pain to remember.

And there were the women. The women of the world will sometimes follow truth longer than anyone else. Even when it appears that truth has been sealed with an irrevocable stone, they will follow to the end. They will mourn for it longer than any other. So a large company of women were helping to prepare the spices and ointments to show final respect to the dead.

It was "black Saturday" indeed. Women wept and men turned their faces from the sky. "Surely there is no hope in heaven," they said. Though heaven had darkened and the earth had shuddered, neither had prevented Calvary. God had not lifted a finger. Good had gone down in defeat. Truth had been crushed to the earth and not one legion of angels had stirred. Surely there is no God. Surely all this talk about the Lord being our shepherd and walking with us through the valley of the shadow is just talk. Let's go back to fishing and making money and trying to go through with this business of living as best we can!

They really believed that all was lost. They were like all of us when we are caught up in the dark web of despair. Life has a way of rolling stones across our way, of sealing tombs tightly, of bringing black Saturdays with their dark hopelessness. There are stones of disappointment bitter and deep—disappointment at what life has done to us, or disappointment at what someone else has done to us. There are stones of frustration, when our fondest hopes have been dashed and we have to stand and look at something that once was beautiful and now is in so many pieces. There are stones of sickness that waste our days and months. There are stones of personal tragedy. A cross hangs in our hearts—a tomb is sealed, and it seems that truth will remain forever on the scaffold and wrong will remain forever on the throne. So we might as well abandon the world to Satan and his angels.

The strong assurance of God is that Black Saturday is but an interlude—a parenthesis. *The day after Calvary is the day before Easter*. Even when the powers of evil boasted of their victory, sat down complacently and assumed that they had the final word, the trumpets were sounding from "the hid battlements of Eternity"[4] and the Son of God was preparing to rise with healing in His wings. Black Saturday was real to them—as it is real to us—but it was all swept away because it is God, and not Satan, who rules the world. The same God who took Jesus Christ out of the tomb and swept Black Saturday into Easter Sunday is the God and Father of us all.

> "It fortifies my soul to know
> That, though I perish, truth is so,
> That, howsoe'er I stray and range,
> Whate'er I do, Thou dost not change.
> I steadier step when I recall
> That, if I slip, Thou dost not fall."[5]

"The doors being shut . . . Jesus came."[6] Satan had slammed the door and turned on his heel to go—thinking matters were done. And with a single sentence Satan fell again as lightning from heaven. There is a splendid note of triumph here. Jesus stood in defiance of all the shut doors of life. The disciples would never be able to forget that moment when the doors were shut and Jesus stood there. Jesus is Lord of death and there are no unfinished symphonies. The keys of death and hell hang at His girdle.[7] Goodness cannot be trampled under heel, but will one day ride terribly and gloriously and triumphantly forth.

ON THE EMMAUS ROAD

There are times when we are shut up in an upper room on a black Saturday. There are also times when we walk the Emmaus Road.[8] The third day after the crucifixion two men left Jerusalem to walk the long road of disappointment. They had seen Calvary and now must go home and pick up the threads of life again. They had "hoped that he was the one to redeem Israel."[9] Says the Gospel record, "While they were talking and discussing together, Jesus himself drew near and went with them."[10] It is an ordinary statement, devoid of drama. Jesus simply drew near and went with them. They were quietly joined by Jesus as unobtrusively as the dust of the Emmaus Road kicked up about their feet. No trumpets were raised and no men in white appeared. Traffic went by as usual. And Jesus drew near. He talked with them and their hearts burned strangely. Then, in the evening candlelight, He broke bread and they recognized Him. And in that recognition, life turned round again. All the hopes of their hearts burst into greater flame.

The Emmaus Road is where most of us walk. It is the road often of broken hopes, of disappointment, of the day's nagging concern. It is life's road. We set out upon it the first day of the week with such high hopes. But by the end of the week, hopes have been broken and good promises lie in fragments. Flowers and stones grow along this road. The Emmaus Road is the road back from Calvary. And Calvary was more real to those two men that day than the open tomb. It is to most of us; for the world has seen more crosses than it has open tombs.

The Emmaus Road is where most of us walk; *and this is where Jesus draws near.* He draws near upon the day's ordinary journey, with its ordinary hopes and its ordinary fears, where the dust of life kicks up about a man's feet.

> "Sometimes a light surprises
> The Christian while he sings;
> It is the Lord, who rises
> With healing in His wings:
> When comforts are declining,
> He grants the soul again
> A season of clear shining,
> To cheer it after rain."[11]

It is the risen Lord—the continuing Christ—who breaks the breads of life with us, breads of sorrow and joy, breads of hope and fear. He is not far from any one of us. Every artist rightly draws the Christ as though He were one of his own land. The Emmaus Road is any road and every road. It runs out from Jerusalem and from Rome and from—where you live.

On that first Easter day, all the trumpets were sounding for Christ. The angels were preparing to crown Him King of kings. But He could not stay. He must hurry back and burst in upon eleven discouraged men who thought all their hopes were forever gone. He must confront Mary Magdalene with the ointment of the dead in her hands. He must join two sad men walking on the road to Emmaus.

Easter will always be a day of high drama, of rolling anthems and of mighty throngs gathered to praise His name. And so it ought to be. But we must hold our crowns for a while. The Christ is not where the glad hallelujahs are ringing. He is on the Emmaus Road. He is looking for a Zacchaeus, or a Matthew, or a Mary Magdalene. He is still gazing upon the multitudes with compassion in His heart. He is by our beds of pain. He is where death has come—busy opening the door to the place prepared for those who love Him. He is still walking the Emmaus Road—a road that runs through your heart and mine, a road that does not stop until it reaches the gates of eternity. And then, perhaps, He will pause and let us crown Him King of kings and Lord of lords.

HE ASCENDED INTO HEAVEN

He is not far from any one of us; and yet the Christian Faith also affirms: "The third day He rose again from the dead; He ascended into heaven." What does this mean? Did He remove Himself from earth completely? The Acts records: "He was lifted up, and a cloud took him out of their sight."[12] It is useless for us to speculate here. These men were human beings who could see only in human terms. Therefore, they saw Him literally taken "up." But what assurance is there in the ascension?

Jesus ascended in order *to re-assume the garments of His majesty*. We say: "He ascended into heaven, and sitteth on the right hand of God the Father Almighty." Now there is no literal right hand, and there is only one God. But this is simply our hungering human attempt to express a truth far greater than our human minds can understand. The Son returned to the Father—the Word returned to the place that was His from the beginning—and assumed all authority in heaven and in earth.

This is what Peter was saying to his Christian readers when he wrote of "Jesus Christ, who has gone into heaven and is at the right hand of God, with angels, authorities, and powers subject to him."[13] This is also what is being said in the letter to the Ephesians which speaks of Jesus Christ raised from the dead and made to sit "at his right hand in the heavenly places, far above all rule and authority and power and dominion."[14] There is no crown great enough to be put upon the head of Christ. He descended into pain and suffering. He ascended into glory and triumph.

Jesus ascended *in order that His Holy Spirit might come to men.* He called His ascension "going away." "It is to your advantage that I go away, for if I do not go away, the Counselor will not come to you; but if I go, I will send him to you."[15] The Counselor, the Comforter, the Holy Spirit, all are names for the Spirit who will come flooding powerfully and more fully back into the world—the Spirit whom every man can touch and be touched by in any place in the world.

He is a Spirit of *comfort,* so He is called the Comforter. It is that Spirit which makes the Christian confident that in life's crises, in the sins which beset us, we can touch Him and His power. Yet He is also a Spirit of judgment, a disturbing Spirit. "When he comes," promised Jesus, "he will convince the world of sin and of righteousness and of judgment."[16] Ever since Jesus ascended into heaven and His Spirit came flooding back into the world, men have felt Him a comfort, but in the sins of their lives they have felt Him a judgment. He remains at once the most comforting presence and the most disturbing presence in all the world.

Jesus ascended in order that He might become *our intercessor.* "We have a great high priest who has passed through the heavens, Jesus, the Son of God."[17] Where the great scales balance, He pleads our case—He who was flesh of our flesh and bone of our bone, who knew the dusty roads of earth, the stabbing pain of betrayal, the lash; who wept at the tomb of a friend and who laughed at a wedding feast. We can have no greater advocate. "For we have not a high priest who is unable to sympathize with our weaknesses, but one who in every respect has been tempted as we are, yet without sin."[18]

"TO PREPARE A PLACE"

The greatest meaning of the ascension is so simple we often forget it. Jesus went away from the earth *to prepare a place for us.* As He said simply to His disciples, "I go to prepare a place for you."[19] Then He added: "And when I go and prepare a place for you, I will come again and will take you to myself, that where I am you may be also."[20] There is needless confusion in the minds of Christians concerning those whom they have loved and lost in Christ. They go immediately to be with Him.

Christ continues—God is with us—beyond death. But the existence of this other world is more easily discussed than described. When we try to imagine what it will be like, our minds are stopped and we find ourselves pathetically imagining in human terms, which are always limited. Will it be as we are now? Will we recognize others? The questions are numerous.

Although it is dangerous to speculate on details, there are some things we are told. And these have been revealed to us by Jesus through the book of Revelation. (The preface of the book reminds us that it is "the revelation of Jesus Christ."[21]) Some of the most beloved revealings about that other world are in the closing chapters 21 and 22.

First, there are certain things not in heaven. Each of these, says Adam Burnet, is like a severing blow at a chain—a chain that holds our minds to all the sorrows of earth.[22]

"The sea was no more."[23] The sea is ever the symbol of separation and mystery. The sea can be a terrible reality of separation from home and ones we love. In that world there shall be no more separation, no more mystery, no more restlessness, no more being tossed about by all the fevers of the world.

"Death shall be no more."[24] There are no periods to man's existence; no more finalities; no more cutting short of life's possibilities; and no cutting down of "the branch that might have grown full straight."[25] Certainly, there will be no more killing and fearsome disease. The grim reaper will have his last harvest.

"There shall no more be anything accursed."[26] From the opening pages of the Bible until the end, we are made aware

of the fact that there is a dark shadow hanging over man—from the time of Eden when Adam looked up into the face of God and said, "No." Nature is not at peace with itself any more than man is at peace with himself. Nature is "red in tooth and claw" and man's inhumanity to man has written a terrible history. But there—there shall be no curse. The curse because of sin will be lifted. Our works shall no longer lie under the blight. Matthew Arnold wrote in his pessimism:

> ". . . most men in a brazen prison live,
>
> . . . .
>
> Their lives to some unmeaning taskwork give,
> Dreaming of naught beyond their prison-wall."[27]

It is a dark pessimism; and there is some truth in it. Mankind does live in a kind of brazen prison; and many give their lives to unmeaning tasks and dream of nothing beyond this prison wall of life. In that World there shall be no curse—no blight. Life will become a joy with God.

"And I saw *no temple in the city,*" says the author of the Revelation.[28] No temple—for there will be no need of a temple! There will be no need of the confession of sin or the agonizing prayer for help or forgiveness. The church and cathedral is the symbol of man's need, his sin and his helplessness. The temple reminds him that he is a broken reed and must seek strength from another world. But in that world there is no need for a temple, "for its temple is the Lord God the Almighty and the Lamb . . . for the Lord God will be their light."[29]

"And night shall be no more."[30] The night is the time of the blackout, the crisis of the sickbed, the often-visit of death. Life is lowest at night; and life's problems become giants to claw at our rest and our peace. The night becomes a symbol of doubt and uncertainty and evil. There shall be no night there.

Positively we can say that beyond death is *vast space and great beauty*. We read of gates of pearl and streets of gold—of jasper walls. So we must take the most precious things of earth to describe poorly the indescribable beauty of that world. Surely the Great Artist who made this world will there dip His brush in lavish colors and outdo even the glory of earth's spring or autumn. If God can do what He has with this broken imperfect world, what will He not do in the glory of His own City!

We get an impression of great space in Revelation 21 and 22. Here is described a City of colossal proportions, fifteen hundred miles high, wide, and long, a perfect cube. Again, the symbols of earth fall short. Jesus said it in a simpler fashion: "In my Father's house are many mansions."[31]

Heaven is a place of *soul-satisfying work*. "His servants shall worship him."[32] The King James Version has "serve" for "worship." But both mean the same in the language of eternity. For pure service to God is pure worship. And pure worship is service. Surely there will be work to do—soul-satisfying, purified, transformed, where powers will be used to the utmost. Perhaps it shall indeed be as Kipling says:

> "They shall splash at a ten-league canvas with
> brushes of comet's hair."[33]

Supremely, heaven is a place *where God is:* "The dwelling of God is with men."[34] It is a place where the creature shall meet his Creator face to face. Shall it then be a face awesome, surrounded by thunders and lightnings? Rather, will it not be the face of Jesus Christ we shall see when we push forward in that multitude around the Throne? And then we shall know, even as also we are known.[35] For we dwell with God.

What happens to the soul immediately after death? It is the Christian faith that the soul goes immediately to be with the Lord, awaiting the resurrection; as Paul says simply, "absent from the body . . . present with the Lord."[36] We can infer that we shall recognize and be recognized. Heaven is not a place of nonentities, where God will have taken some great sponge and wiped away our personalities until we are all one great blur. I will be I, and you will be you. Of course we cannot answer all the questions that arise here. "Beloved, now are we the sons of God," says John; and then he stops before unanswered questions: "and it doth not yet appear what we shall be: but we know that, when he shall appear, we shall be like him; for we shall see him as he is."[37] And Paul, trying to peer ahead into that world, said: "Eye hath not seen, nor ear heard, neither have entered into the heart of man, the things which God hath prepared for them that love him."[38]

In the assurance of another world, shall we despise this world or turn our backs upon it? Some have. Some have said, "This is a world of pain. I will have nothing to do with it." But we remember that Christ came into this world. He spoke of that other world and pointed our hopes toward it; but He never despised this world. In spite of its pain, He challenged men to regard life as a sacred trust. The assurance of heaven is not given to justify us in turning our backs upon this world, but to enable us to live in this world with courage and faith. Christ continues to walk the roads of this world in His Spirit. He blesses where men will touch Him in prayer's conversation. He lifts where men will grasp His hand in faith. With the Christ who continues with us we shall live here as gallantly and as courageously and as faithfully as we can—until the banners of this life, stained and torn, are proudly furled in the halls of the Kingdom of Heaven.

This is the continuing Christ. He continues with us in life and beyond death. He walks the Emmaus Roads of hopelessness and appears in the upper rooms of despair. He is. He is power and peace; and to touch Him is to know power and peace. "Let us then with confidence draw near to the throne of grace, that we may receive mercy and find grace to help in time of need."[39]

"For the moment all discipline seems painful rather than pleasant; later it yields the peaceful fruit of righteousness to those who have been trained by it."

Hebrews 12:11

PART TWO

THE STRONG DISCIPLINE

"That low man seeks a little thing to do,
Sees it and does it:
This high man, with a great thing to pursue,
Dies ere he knows it."

ROBERT BROWNING
"A Grammarian's Funeral"

CHAPTER V

The Discipline of Faith

> "But they that wait upon the Lord shall renew their strength; they shall mount up with wings as eagles; they shall run, and not be weary; and they shall walk, and not faint."
>
> *Isaiah* 40:31 (K.J.V.)

> "Lord, I believe; help thou mine unbelief."
>
> *Mark* 9:24 (K.J.V.)

IT IS not enough to affirm that God has come down to us upon the level of our needs and has given us strong assurance that He is a God of mercy and concern. We have said little or nothing about our part in all this. Where do we meet God to find that power and peace which He is willing to give? Where is the trysting place of God and man? There is only one answer: *Man meets God upon the level of his faith.* The discipline of faith is the price of peace of mind and power in living.

The word "discipline" comes from the same word as "disciple" or "learner." Discipline has been defined as that "training which corrects, molds, strengthens, or perfects."[1] So the discipline of faith is learning to live in God's world with God. This discipline does indeed correct, mold, strengthen, and perfect. The power in daily living that this faith brings is not acquired overnight. It is a discipline—a "learning"—of the years.

"THEY WHO WAIT FOR THE LORD"

Faith is ever a strenuous discipline. For it is not a matter of glib formulas or even of intellectual assent. "They who wait for the Lord shall renew their strength."[2] The Hebrew word for "wait" is a strong word. It also means to be bound. The picture in the word is of a man chained to the place where he is, and able to do nothing but wait for God.

Waiting on God means the trampling of doubts under heel—believing where there is perhaps nothing to believe—hoping when there is not even a shred to go on—praying in a void, without words, a lifting up of the spirit unto God. Faith is surrender in its most absolute sense. And this is not easy. It is a strenuous, daily discipline.

Yet this strenuous discipline does yield its results. It is a *gracious* discipline—one that brings power in living.

> "They who wait for the Lord shall renew their
> strength,
> they shall mount up with wings like eagles,
> they shall run and not be weary,
> they shall walk and not faint."[3]

We feel, of course, that it should be the other way around—walking, then running, and finally soaring. But in the language of faith the sequence here is correct. Soaring comes occasionally. We all have "mountaintop" experiences. Running in a great burst of speed comes occasionally also. But walking daily and not fainting in this business of living is the thing we must learn to do all the time.

You can trip people who run, and bring down to earth those who soar; but you can do nothing with the man who has learned to walk steadily, steadfastly, purposefully in the heat of the day and the dark of the night—who believes that God is with him. Lord Rosebery in his life of Thomas Chalmers, the man who led the fight to free the Scottish Church from the state, wrote: "Here was a man . . . who had the dust and fire of the world on his clothes, but who carried with him his shrine everywhere."[4] This is the secret of great faith—not to avoid the dust and fire of the world, but to walk through it carrying a shrine.

The most effective spirits have been those who have committed themselves to the rock of belief that we are not playthings of the cosmos, but that God turns a face of mercy and concern toward us; that for all its pain, life lived sincerely under Him is not without meaning and not without victory. They have believed that life possesses meaning only when it is lived on a plane of faith not fear, love not selfishness, hope not doubt, graciousness not cynicism. To this discipline of faith God calls us.

FAITH AND CONVICTIONS

Part of the daily discipline of a great faith is to stand for the right. When we meet God on the level of faith, more often than not it is an encounter where God requires that we stand in our place for the right. It has been said that there is one funeral long overdue today, and that is the funeral of the so-called innocent bystander. He no longer exists, of course. No one is an innocent bystander today. Our times are upon us and must be faced with the discipline of faith in God who requires that we stand for the right.

The tasks that face us are giant's tasks indeed. The world is divided into two basic ideologies. Although the problem of world Communism is now worn thin upon many a pulpit and lecture platform, the truth is that the problem is with us and will probably be with us for a long time to come. Communism challenges every Christian to examine the bases of his faith and the depth of his convictions. Communism has again called the Christian Faith out into the arena with the lions. But Communism is an idea and not a lion; and it will be defeated only by another idea greater and stronger.

There is before us the problem of the races, the problem of living with one another. This problem is highlighted in certain places, such as the southern United States and South Africa, but actually it is a problem everywhere. Every Christian must undergo the discipline of facing this problem, and of deciding out of his own convictions what he must do and how he must conduct himself.

But what about the little fretting problems of the day? When drums are rolling and flags are flying, then perhaps we can summon the courage to live bravely. But when we are called to be Christian in the humdrum tasks of the day, that is another matter. Yet the decision to do right in the little battles may be worth more than the fighting of a hundred gallant battles upon the field where all may see. Whether we face great tasks or little crises, our Christian faith must undergo the daily discipline of decision for the right, as well as the discipline of complete trust. No man changes his time by condemning it or by running away from it—he can change it only by standing in his place under God. This is part of the constant discipline of a great faith.

FAITH'S GREATEST HOUR

But faith reaches its greatest hour when it says: "I believe, although I cannot prove." *The discipline of great faith also calls us to stand, when there is nothing else to be done.* The Bible has many great examples, but one of the most notable is Isaiah in besieged Jerusalem.[5] The scene is one of the most striking in the Bible. The armies of Assyria have conquered all of Judah and are now besieging Jerusalem.

> "The Assyrian came down like the wolf on the fold,
> And his cohorts were gleaming with purple and gold."[6]

Lord Byron has described it poetically, but it was not a poetic occasion. Rather it was a grim time. A besieged city of ancient times was a place of horror; and for Jerusalem with her meager water supply, it was unbearable. "This day is a day of distress, of rebuke, and of disgrace," said King Hezekiah.

Then in a sentence, he described the agony of the situation: "Children have come to the birth, and there is no strength to bring them forth."[7]

The Rabshakeh, the commander in chief of the Assyrian armies, had stood outside the walls and hurled this question at the defenders on the walls: "On whom do you now rely?"[8] It was a hard question to answer. Force of arms had failed. Diplomatic intrigue and alliances with Egypt had failed. In vain they had looked for many anxious weeks for the appearance of the Egyptian war chariots. So Hezekiah turned to Isaiah: "Lift up your prayer for the remnant that is left."[9]

This was and always is faith's greatest hour. For faith's greatest hour comes when the issue is in doubt, and when it appears that all is lost. Faith's greatest hour comes when it must answer the question: "On whom do you now rely?" And only faith had something to say that day to the taunts of the Assyrian. Indeed, faith is the only thing that does have anything to say when the black hour comes. So out of a deep well of amassed spiritual resources, out of hours of prayer, out of great moments in worship, out of a life lived courageously under God, from Isaiah there came the answer: "Thus says the Lord: Do not be afraid."[10]

This answer of faith came out of the years, not out of the moment. Creeds are not manufactured; they are carved from experience. The creed of a great faith is one of the last things to come out of a man's life. Paul put this down after years of following Christ: "For I know whom I have believed and I am sure that he is able to guard until that Day what has been entrusted to me."[11] And out of the years of living with God, Isaiah calmly affirmed in the chaos of a city about to fall to the invader: "Do not be afraid."

The taunting question of the Assyrian commander in chief has been heard across the centuries. "On whom do you now rely?" He is anti-God, anti-faith, the believer in horses and chariots, the believer in what he can see. He gives aid and comfort to those who plan their lives upon purely materialistic lines. If he stood before us today, he would probably sneer: "Where do you Christians get all this about faith? What other God is there besides money, votes, and power?"

Those with an empty or halfhearted religion have been forced to endure the humiliation of having nothing to answer when the crisis comes. Those who have failed to amass the resources of faith through the years have nothing to answer when the invader of doubt and crisis stands before the walls. So great faith calls for discipline through the years—the discipline of walking and "learning" daily with God. Those with that faith know the glory of that shining, tremulous hour when the soul is steadfast although the body calls for the flag to be hauled down in surrender. Just before facing a serious operation, the father of Justice William O. Douglas told his son: "If I die it will be glory; if I live it will be grace."[12] This is the answer of faith, when crisis stands before the walls.

Such faith has tremendous power: "And the angel of the Lord went forth . . ."[13] The Assyrian army was routed overnight; but there is more to this than the dispersal of the Assyrian army. History records disasters that have been visited upon armies and have forced them to retreat. The point that we must not miss is the juxtaposition of two things here—the faith of Isaiah and the dispersal of the Assyrians. This was a faith that called down "the angel of the Lord."

At such faith, God came down—broke in upon the tedious history of man as if to say, "I shall go down upon Jerusalem and they shall know that faith is greater than unbelief, love is greater than hate; and that the fear of God is greater than horses and chariots."

Centuries later, evil ran rampant. Injustice paid off in Roman coin. But men and women of faith were still praying. And God came down again—broke in upon the city of Man in the person of His Son. God pushed open the doors of the years and stood Himself upon the threshold: "I shall go down among them, and they shall know that faith and love and hope are not idle dreams, but part of the very fabric of eternity." And the armies of Satan have been in retreat from that hour.

"On whom do you now rely?" It is Hell's question; and Hell deserves an answer. The answer comes from the deep wells of a great faith disciplined—"learned"—through the years. And Hell shall ever tremble at that faith; for in response to it God comes down upon His people.

FAITH WITHOUT BOUNDARY

"And nothing will be impossible to you . . ."[14] The faith of Jesus Christ also calls to the seemingly impossible. *Jesus calls us to the discipline of a faith that knows no boundary.* We stand in admiration at the audacity of the statement. On the surface, it sounds like the mouthings of a starry-eyed idealist. Actually it came out of the fires of a desperate life situation. It is a challenge thrown down in the very heat of life—as faith always is.

There was an agonized father and his stricken son, an unbelieving and jeering crowd, and nine chagrined and ashamed disciples. They had been unable to help the father and his son. "Why?" they asked Jesus. The answer came bluntly: "Because of your little faith." Then, as if that rebuke were not enough, there came this breath-taking challenge: "For truly, I say to you, if you have faith as a grain of mustard seed, you will say to this mountain, 'Move hence to yonder place,' and it will move; and nothing will be impossible to you."[15]

(This rebuke was not to the crowd, but to the disciples of Christ. We come to the point sometimes when we cannot count on our name as Christians or on our committees and organizations to save us or to make any kind of impact on the world. The world was never saved in a committee meeting. Neither was a city saved merely by a sign in front of a church.)

Let the rebuke stand and look at something else here. For there is more than a rebuke in this remarkable statement. Here is *something that refuses to know a boundary.* "If you have faith . . . nothing will be impossible to you." Try to put a boundary around that!

Now of course the supercilious and skeptic will attempt to throw a boundary around it, and mutter something about having "stars in your eyes." There is such a thing as a facile idealism—a looking at the world through rose-colored glasses, blithely assuming that everything must be all right. But Jesus Christ was no more a facile idealist than He was a supercilious skeptic. He was no idle dreamer; and no one could ever accuse Him of looking at the world through rose-colored glasses. Indeed, no man ever faced the crises of life more realistically, and no man ever had to face more, than Jesus Christ. He was talking here about a faith clearly focused upon God, and that is a different matter: If you have faith in God—who knows no horizons or fixed mountains, and who is not bound by the chains of time and circumstance.

Always this kind of faith is a continuous adventure. This ship never puts in at port, never hauls down its flag, except at Heaven's port. This kind of faith is something to be cast down into the dust of the earth, where a father agonizes over his son. In the Bible, faith is not a noun; it is a verb —not a sitting-still but a going-out. Beethoven used to go out into the country with a piece of blank paper in his hand and come back with music. He believed the music was there and went out to find out. Abraham went out to find the City of God. Isaiah stood firm in the face of Assyria and believed God greater. Paul refused to know a horizon but "pressed on" to the high calling of God. John in his old age refused to know a horizon: "We are God's children now; it does not yet appear what we shall be."[16] The children of God know no horizon in life or death. They are called to move forward where they cannot see, even into the dark. "Yet the dark too," said Browning, "is God."[17] They stand audaciously before mountains.

Halford E. Luccock has reminded us of that dramatic incident in Harold Lamb's life of Alexander the Great when the maps gave out before the towering Himalayas and Alexander's army was thrown into confusion. They had literally "marched off the map."[18] Faith is always marching off the map. At that point, Jesus dares us to raise our banners and move forward—assuring us that upon such faith more than mountains have been moved.

"If you have faith as a grain of mustard seed . . ."; we are not called to the spectacular, to throwing ourselves off the pinnacle of the Temple. The discipline of faith is strenuous, but God will be content with even a small portion! Even an upward look is not lost, nor is this humble prayer scorned: "I believe; help thou mine unbelief."[19]

George Santayana reminds us that

> "Columbus found a world and had no chart,
> Save one that faith deciphered in the skies."[20]

So faith reaches a time when it has no charts, save those deciphered in the skies of God. Isaiah within embattled Jerusalem is an inspiration. But there is one Voice that brings courage to the arm and hope to the eye: "If you have faith as a grain of mustard seed . . . nothing will be impossible to you." And we must pray: "Lord, I believe. I have some faith. Yet there are some parts of me unconquered, some places unsubdued, some things unsubmitted. Lord, I believe. But, O Thou who knowest our frame, who rememberest that we are dust, help Thou mine unbelief." Faith, too, is a part of God's strong comfort.

CHAPTER VI

The Great Antagonist

"He who believes in God . . . stands under God's commands."

KARL BARTH[1]

MAN meets God upon the level of his faith. But this meeting is not always a place of peace and light. Rather, it is sometimes a place of battle; for God is the Great Antagonist of much that is in our souls. Real faith is forged when creature meets Creator and knows that he is creature—when unholiness meets Holiness and knows sin.

THE MAN AND THE THRONE

Faith must see a Throne. Upon that throne sits a holy King whose holiness is antagonistic to our sin, and whose sovereignty is antagonistic to all that earth calls secure. The classic example is in the sixth chapter of Isaiah. Isaiah enters the Temple to pray—at a time of great national crisis, and probably for him great personal crisis also. The great Uzziah is dead. The king who had brought Judah to the peak of prosperity and power has died as a leper, after having committed the sacrilege of trying to take the place of the high priest. Isaiah's world has collapsed. Everything that he had counted upon as secure has shifted from under him like treacherous sand.

The great point of Isaiah 6 is that Isaiah saw a Throne eternally occupied by the King of heaven and earth. Thereafter he was never doubtful about who held the ultimate issues. Yet that vision threw him to his knees in sudden horror: "Woe is me! For I am lost; for I am a man of unclean lips . . ."[2] What had driven Isaiah to his knees was the realization of the yawning gulf between what he was and what God was. This is where a true sense of sin is born. At the same time that faith knows the power of the Lord God, faith also knows its own unrighteousness.

Who then can bridge that awful gap? Faith can only raise a penitent cry; it is God who must bridge the gap. It is God who must dispatch the angel of grace with the burning coal of forgiveness: "And he touched my mouth, and said: 'Behold, this has touched your lips; your guilt is taken away, and your sin forgiven.' "[3]

Now faith is ready for its committal: "Here I am! Send me."[4] This is in part a committal of gratitude—the gratitude of a man who knows God's grace. But it is more a *committal in faith*. Isaiah has seen a Throne that will never be empty, and he is now ready to commit himself in faith's adventure. He is willing to be "sent," to be thrust out into the world. Faith knows no more what is coming tomorrow than does unfaith—but faith has this: the belief that tomorrow is in God's hands.

Faith that does not see a Throne, and its own unrighteousness and God's forgiving grace, is not faith. Faith must pass through some such experience of discipline, or else it is merely the parroter of phrases. The phrases of faith take on meaning after a man has himself seen a Throne, and felt the burning coal from off the altar of God. When a man knows that he has gone down to his house justified in the sight of God, he is a man ready to commit himself to God. The Christian believes that a coal has been taken from off the high altar of God and laid upon the lips of man, even Jesus Christ the Lamb slain. The gap has been bridged in Him. Our faith is forged in the experience of that grace.

THE GOD OF PENIEL

But faith does not always have a "temple" experience. Faith must sometimes wrestle with God in a dark night of the soul and be smitten to its knees. Sometimes we must wrestle with God, like Jacob at the ford of the river Jabbok.[5] Jacob has now turned homeward again, after nearly twenty years. Between him and home is the fierce Esau, now a Bedouin sheik with many warriors. Jacob finds himself at the ford of the river, on the day before he is to meet Esau. How would Esau receive the man who had stolen his birthright? Jacob remembered that Esau had sworn an oath to be avenged. The past was now catching up.

The issue of the morrow is still in doubt. Unable to sleep, Jacob walks in lonely meditation beside the river. "And Jacob was left alone,"[6] turned in upon himself in silent and humiliating examination of his own inner resources.

"And there wrestled a man with him."[7] Out of the darkness of his own extremity, there came a silent Antagonist who grappled for his very soul. These two met in that struggle which always takes place when God confronts the soul of a man and demands an answer.

Finally, after a desperate night-long struggle, such as is known only to those who wrestle with God, a strange thing happened: Jacob would not let go. He began to cling with desperate earnestness. "I will not let you go, unless you bless me."[8] There is deep meaning here. Jacob was not a shallow man, and neither was he a coward. He realized that the time had arrived to come to grips with God. He dared not let God go, without a blessing. So his cry was the cry of a deeply disturbed soul. Matters were not right. He must see this thing through. Charles Wesley has a hymn in which can be heard this cry of Jacob:

> "Yield to me now, for I am weak,
> But confident in self-despair;
> Speak to my heart, in blessing speak;
> Be conquered by my instant prayer."[9]

But Jacob was not ready to receive his blessing. Matters were not right between him and God. Hence the real struggle had just begun. God had a question to put to Jacob that was far more withering than the hand that had touched his thigh. This question would touch his soul: "And he said to him, 'What is your name?' "[10] This question went straight to Jacob's soul, and he was forced to his humiliating answer —in one word. The word no doubt came haltingly, as the last line of defense is breached stone by stone. So did this word fall from Jacob's lips like a stone: " 'What is your name?' And he said, 'Jacob.' "[11] Jacob in Hebrew means "trickster" or "supplanter." So the saying of his name was a confession: "My name is Jacob—the Trickster, the Supplanter, the one who puts himself ahead of everyone else, who lied to his father, tricked his brother, cheated his father-in-law."

God's question to Jacob withered more than his thigh; it withered his pride and selfishness. So God forces a man to look at himself. Two natures can war in the soul. Faith is forged when humble confession is made and the good wins through. The dust of this terrible conflict of the soul is never seen; but it is the greatest of all battles.

"Your name shall no more be called Jacob, but Israel."[12] Jacob could now receive his blessing—a new name and a changed heart. He was no longer Jacob the Supplanter, but Israel the Prince of God. "And . . . the sun rose upon him"—a simple and beautiful expression.[13] Never does the sun arise in such beauty as on that day when a man has wrestled with God and has been preserved. "So Jacob called the name of the place Peniel, saying, 'For I have seen God face to face, and yet my life is preserved.' "[14]

Peniel means "the face of God." At Peniel we meet God face to face and alone. Peniel turns us in upon ourselves in silent and humiliating examination. Pretenses must be stripped off, as when the African medicine man who came near his death took off his amulets and charms and flung them into the sea with the words, "Now I will be a man and meet my God alone." And when we meet Him, His question is the same: "What is your name?" If we answer honestly, we are left defenseless. Something is loosened within us that once had a tight grip. Something is melted down that once was hard as granite. But here is the blessed paradox: To prevail with God is to yield to Him:

> "My will is not my own
> Till Thou hast made it Thine;
> If it would reach a monarch's throne
> It must its crown resign."[15]

We must admit that we are Jacobs, before God can make us Israels.

But does this Antagonist remain forever in the shadows? Who is He that grapples with my soul and makes me see things I do not wish to see, and confess things that I have stopped a thousand times from coming out? What face and form does He wear? Our Antagonist, our Blessed Adversary, that Silent Presence who stands over against us and demands an answer, wears the face and form of Jesus Christ. It is He with whom we grapple and with whom we have to do. It is Jesus Christ who is the Blessed Antagonist and the Hound of Heaven, who is both judgment and mercy. His judgment reduces us to the dust. His mercy lifts us to the stars. It is Jesus Christ whom we meet at our Peniels. The sword must be given up to Him. Only He can write a new and shining name upon our hearts.

ENCOUNTER WITH CHRIST

An encounter with Jesus Christ can be the most electric encounter of a man's life. A meeting with Christ is a meeting with a Divine Antagonist, whose love is both holy and fierce.

Once Jesus was passing through Jericho. It could have been any town—or our town. The crowds gathered around Him, as crowds would do now. But Jesus was never moved by crowds—except with compassion. He fed crowds, but He did not attempt to sway crowds. He dealt with individuals.

So we should not be surprised to see Him look up and "see" Zacchaeus perched in that now famous sycamore tree.

What did Jesus see? Possibly He saw a wistful figure of a man—not the usual villain of the mustache and the leer, but a pathetic and wistful little man who was disposed to bluster at times to cover up his feelings of inferiority. Jesus probably saw a lonely man, despised and hated by his countrymen as a quisling, an outcast dressed in the clothes of the rich. Even his name mocked him; for Zacchaeus means "the righteous one," and Zacchaeus was anything but righteous.

Pity cannot wash the spots away from Zacchaeus—or any man. He was not above fraud. He was a publican, a tax collector; and an honest tax collector in those days was hard to find. Long ago Zacchaeus had given up the luxury of having pretensions about himself. He knew what he was and so did everyone else.

Jesus looked up and "saw" Zacchaeus and deliberately invited Himself into the man's life: "Zacchaeus, make haste and come down; for I must stay at your house today."[16] And a gasp must have gone up from the crowd. This was the last thing a respected teacher like Jesus was expected to do. They all "murmured." "He has gone in to be guest of a man who is a sinner."[17] Would the Messiah and Son of God sit down with sinners? He is certainly in the wrong place today!

This is precisely one of the thundering points of this old story of Zacchaeus and Jesus. Jesus was in the wrong place. To all intents and purposes, by all the standards of His day and ours, Jesus was in the wrong place. If Jesus had drawn a sword and gone charging after the nearest Roman official, no one would have thought anything of it probably. As a matter of fact, some in that crowd would have applauded and drawn swords of their own and followed Him. But to accept the invitation, nay, to invite oneself into the home of a sinner—this was impossible!

Yet this is what God is forever doing—going after and receiving the unlikely. Jacob was a thief and a liar. And

Jesus was forever receiving the most unlikely people, gathering them about Himself, going to them, accepting invitations to eat with them, and breaking the Sabbath laws if He felt He could help someone. So the Bible is the story of the redemption of the unlikely. Jesus believed that they that are sick have need of a physician; and so He went to them and grappled with them, as God grappled with Jacob.

AN ELECTRIC ENCOUNTER

When Jesus and Zacchaeus met, it was an electric encounter. Zacchaeus sat at table with *someone who cared nothing for money, power, or fame.* And certainly money and power formed the cornerstones of Zacchaeus' life. He was used to moving in circles where money, power, and fame were the things. He possibly had invited that day the Roman official of the town, some other of the publicans. These were all men who dressed well, and were men of power. But the eyes of Jesus passed over that array of wealth as though it were not there at all. Zacchaeus thought: "This is Someone different." He was stirred. Rudyard Kipling in an address to the students of McGill University, Montreal, said: "Some day you will meet a man who cares nothing for money, power, or fame, and then you will know how poor you are." Zacchaeus met such a Man that day. He knew, perhaps for the first time, how poor he was.

Zacchaeus sat at table that day with *someone of intense faith.* His eyes were steady, His countenance was clear. He was never glancing over His shoulder to see the flash of an assassin's dagger. Zacchaeus probably had guards posted. No doubt he feared to walk alone by night. Yet here was someone who sat calmly, while rumors were flying thick and fast that the highest rulers in Palestine were seeking His life. Zacchaeus knew again how poor he was.

But then also, Zacchaeus sat at table with someone who could look into his eyes and *assure him of forgiveness.* Zacchaeus was a "son of Abraham"; yet the sense of sin was with him—a constant sense of not being on the right footing with God. His tensions and anxieties were but symptoms of a deeper sickness. Now here is someone who says, "Zacchaeus, your sins can be forgiven."

In a word, Zacchaeus had encountered God—not as an angel of light or a whirling pillar of fire. Let Hollywood keep its God in cinemascope and stereophonic sound! The God of the Bible is the God in Jesus Christ who invites Himself into my heart, sits down at table, and brings salvation to my house.

A STERN ENCOUNTER

Now this encounter was not all sweetness and light. Rather, it was a stern encounter. When Zacchaeus realized how poor he was, how much he needed in the way of faith to make his way through the world, and how desperately he needed a sense of forgiveness, there was a transformation. The possibility of having these things was now open before him. "And Zacchaeus stood and said to the Lord, 'Behold, Lord, the half of my goods I give to the poor; and if I have defrauded any one of anything, I restore it fourfold.' "[18] The path of salvation is always paved with the stones of penitence and of restitution. When God encounters the soul, He does not sign a contract. Salvation is penitence without expectation of reward. God will not despise a broken and a contrite heart. So Jesus said: "Today salvation has come to this house."[19]

"For the Son of man came to seek and to save the lost."[20] This was His answer to the question of the crowd: "Why did you go into the house of Zacchaeus?" Strange that God must be forever telling us why He came to earth. When great men come to visit, they sit in high places; but when God came He took off His shoes and His crown and He sat at tables with the lowly and needy in soul.

An encounter with God in Jesus Christ is surgery of the keenest sort—a cutting off of pretension, a call for penitence and restitution. But it is also blessing—a restoration of soul and true peace of mind. So God grapples with us at our fords of Jabbok and calls to us sitting in our sycamore trees: "Come down from your wistful observations. I must stay at your house today. . . . Behold I stand at the door and knock; if any one hears my voice and opens the door, I will come in to him and eat with him, and he with me."[21] Lloyd Douglas has this conversation between Zacchaeus and Jesus: "Zacchaeus," said the carpenter gently, "what did you see that made you desire this peace?" "Good master—I saw—mirrored in your eyes—the face of the Zacchaeus I was meant to be!"[22] When we sit down with Jesus, we see the man we were meant to be.

CHAPTER VII

The Great Decision

> "All Christianity concentrates on the man at the crossroads . . . The true philosophy is concerned with the instant. Will a man take this road or that? —that is the only thing to think about, if you enjoy thinking."
>
> G. K. CHESTERTON[1]

THE Christian Faith calls for decision. A man who contemplates this Faith eventually stands at the crossroads where the soul is tried and decision is made. Christianity presents a cross which must be carried or left lying. It presents a Saviour who must be received or rejected. This decision is part of the strong discipline of the Christian Faith.

"ALL THE KING'S MEN"

An illustration from the Old Testament is one of its most thought-provoking stories—the story of Naaman being commanded by Elisha to wash in the Jordan.[2] Naaman was commander-in-chief of the Syrian armies—and a leper. The king of Syria snatched at any straw to save his valuable general. When he heard that there was a prophet in Israel who might cure a man of leprosy, he sent Naaman to Elisha.

There is something quite arresting about the spectacle of Naaman coming to Elisha. The Syrian general's banners and pennants were flying before him. Wagons carried ten talents of silver, six thousand pieces of gold, and ten changes of raiment as a present for Elisha. All this Naaman was prepared to cast into the scales that he might be clean. We are reminded of the old nursery rhyme:

> "Humpty Dumpty sat on a wall,
> Humpty Dumpty had a great fall;
> All the king's horses and all the king's men
> Couldn't put Humpty together again."

Now nothing could have come as a greater shock to Naaman than the message from Elisha that he must go and wash seven times in the river Jordan—if he wished to be clean. Naaman's pride had already been severely wounded by the fact that Elisha had refused to come in person. But now this idea of dipping in the muddy Jordan was unthinkable—especially for a general, and probably a five-star general at that!

"COULD I NOT WASH IN THEM?"

Naaman's reaction as well as his anger was quite human. Surely there must be an easier way to accomplish the same purpose. He had thought that surely Elisha would wave his hand over the affected place and the leprosy would disappear. But then, if one must wash in a river, why not the Abana and Pharpar rivers at home, instead of this muddy Jordan? "Are not Abana and Pharpar, the rivers of Damascus, better than all the waters of Israel?" thought Naaman. "Could I not wash in them, and be clean?"[3] The Abana and Pharpar were two very beautiful rivers, rising high in the mountains above Syria and flowing through a beautiful gorge down into the city of Damascus. They were inestimable sources of charm and fertility.

Why not Abana and Pharpar? Why not a more palatable substitute? Again, Naaman's reaction is the human reaction *when confronted with the discipline of real religion.* The current rising tide of interest in religion reaches its peak in the diligent search for "peace of mind." But peace cannot be secured without discipline. There is peace of mind to be found in the Christian Faith—but there is also discipline. There is a security in Christianity—but there is also discipline. Prayer's disciplines cannot be avoided. The Bible is not a handbook to personal salvation, but the Word of God that penetrates to joint and marrow. Worship is not a convention, but a preparation to do battle. These have no substitute. Faith brings its rich rewards, but also its strong discipline.

"WASHING IN JORDAN"

All this is to say that the "Jordan" is there, and if we will be "clean," we must wash in it. "Washing in Jordan" calls for *subjection to authority*. Naaman was a man of the military. He understood subjection to authority and obedience to command. There comes a time in every man's life when, if he is to know real religion, he must bow to God his creator. This is not an easy thing to do. "What lack I yet?" asks the world, crowding into the churches for healing and peace of mind. The time has come for the Church to say: "You lack subjection to the authority of the Lord God."

Washing in Jordan calls for *effort*. Simply, Naaman had to move from where he was and go down into the Jordan. He could not stand there and let Elisha come out and wave his hand over the place and pronounce a few magic words, be cleansed, and then get back in his chariot and go home. It was not as simple as that. He had to go down into the Jordan himself. He had to do something! Someone has said that a religion that does nothing, that gives nothing, that costs nothing, that suffers nothing, is worth nothing. Our fathers used to pray, "O Lord, we have left undone that which we ought to have done." Their children do not feel the lack. We could possibly confess our sins of commission, but might be honestly bewildered to make a list of our sins of omission. We are used to having religion do something for us, while we do little for or on account of religion.

Only the *humble* wash in Jordan. It required nothing less than humility for Naaman to strip off his medals and armor, lay aside his sword; and then, with nothing, go down into the river. So does the Christian Faith call for us to deliver up our sword—to strip off those encrustments that we show before the world, and show God humility of spirit. No man can become clean until he does. No man can become clean until he realizes that neither ten talents of silver nor six thousand pieces of gold nor ten changes of raiment can save him.

Again, washing in Jordan calls for *faith*. We collide with the word at every turn in the Christian religion. When Naaman dipped in the Jordan, it was above all else a signal act of faith. He had come to the point where, without a single battalion at his back, he had to walk into the Jordan. That is faith. The morning does not usually bring a Gideon's fleece[4] to guide us. There is just the day with its demands, with its possibility of failure, with its crises and its call to walk in faith. The Christian Faith says, "Come! Not for healing first, or for peace of mind first, but come and know the discipline of putting your faith in the Lord God. Know the discipline and the reward of stepping out day after day in that faith—without written proof, without guarantee."

There is no substitute for the disciplines of real religion. Abana and Pharpar will not do. Wash in the Jordan or remain unclean. Naaman was an angry man, but he had sense enough to know that he had better try the Jordan. Can you not imagine that years afterward this thought would cross Naaman's mind: "Suppose I had refused the word of the prophet?"

There is an oft-told story that when the great organist at Freiburg Cathedral became too old to play, they made him the custodian of the organ. He was instructed that no one was to touch the organ except the regular organist. One day a stranger presented himself at the cathedral and asked to play the great organ. The custodian at first refused, but after much pleading, he gave his reluctant consent. The story is that the old church never rang with such magnificent music as on that day. And when the stranger finished, the custodian asked his name. The stranger replied, "I am Felix Mendelssohn." Long years afterward, the custodian would tell the story and then end with this, "Felix Mendelssohn! And to think I almost refused to let him play!" Long years afterward, Naaman looked at his clean flesh and said to any who would listen to him, "That muddy Jordan! And to think I almost refused to go down!"

There is a constant Jordan in the Christian religion. Its disciplines are real and stringent. Its rewards are great. There is an abiding Saviour—He who can take the shattered fragments of a man's life and put them back together again, who can speak the word of peace when angry waves are breaking over a man's soul. But His discipline is real. His cross is real—and waits for us to pick it up or walk over it and follow what appears to be an easy path. So many have said in wonderment in later years: "Jesus Christ—and to think I almost refused to let Him touch my life!"

"LET HIM TAKE UP HIS CROSS"

When Jesus Christ touches our lives, He stands before the Jordan. At His feet lies a cross. There is one saying of Jesus that must have cost Him many followers: "If any man would come after me, let him deny himself and take up his cross and follow me."[5] There is not a word that tries a man's soul more, or that makes him search it more deeply. The discipline of bearing the cross is the sternest discipline of the faith. Here God the Great Antagonist of the soul meets man, not in the cool of a garden, but at the foot of a cross where "old Jordan" rolls.

He who believes that the Christian Faith is only a prescription for peace, prosperity, and success in this world is living in a fool's paradise. Jesus first spoke of bearing a cross to twelve men who were walking in a fool's paradise of over-confidence and not a little pride. They had followed Him and listened to His teaching, had seen the sick healed and the dead raised. They had observed His deft and masterly encounters with His enemies. His authority and pre-eminence were unquestioned in their minds. No doubt they could visualize themselves already seated upon thrones, and had already had private discussions among themselves about who should occupy the chief seats in His Kingdom.

It came as a distinct shock when He began to speak not of a throne but of a cross; not of His coronation but of His crucifixion. This could not be! So Peter took Him aside: "God forbid, Lord! This shall never happen to you."[6] This is not in the character of the Messiah. "Speak to us of legions of angels, of the unseating of Rome, of the establishment of a righteous Kingdom. But do not speak to us of death and suffering."

Then it was, after severely rebuking Peter, that our Lord must have drawn away a little—from the twelve and from the crowd which had gathered. With great frankness, He laid before them without stint the cost of following Him: "If any man would come after me, let him . . . take up his cross."[7] Let us not draw the teeth of this, or attempt to smooth its cutting edges. For Jesus was not necessarily speaking of the ordinary distresses and problems of life which come to us all and which we sometimes call crosses—"the thousand natural shocks that flesh is heir to."[8] If this were all, then the saying would have been superfluous even for the twelve apostles and the listening crowd. Were they not human, and therefore were they not already bearing the crosses of human distress and problems? Surely Jesus was speaking of something else—of the voluntary, deliberate act of taking up something *which we do not have to take up.*

THE FURNITURE OF THE CROSS

What then is the furniture of this cross which Jesus bids us bear as we follow in His train? *Faith* is in that cross. Real faith is a cross—a life-long cross. Its nails pierce. Its Golgotha blackness is real. Faith is the soul-searing discipline of living without proof, with no absolute certainty that the battle will be won. Faith is a cross on a hill. Faith is crying, "My God, my God, why hast thou forsaken me?"[9]

Love is part of the furniture of that cross. Can love be a cross? Christian love is ever the taking of a cross: "Love is patient and kind; love is not jealous or boastful; it is not arrogant or rude. Love does not insist on its own way; it is not irritable or resentful . . . Love bears all things, believes all things, hopes all things, endures all things."[10] Love is the denial of self—"let him deny himself"—or as Tyndale translates it with a note of iron: "Let him forsake himself." Christian love calls for a man to become a stranger to himself and his own desires. Love is the crucifixion of self. Love is praying: "Father, forgive them; for they know not what they do."[11]

This kind of love is not *eros,* or the Hollywood kind of love. Neither is it *filia,* or a mild kind of brotherly affection. The New Testament and Christian word for love is *agape* —the strong love that sent Christ to the cross. Agape forsakes itself for others. Agape is the crucifixion of self.

We are not done with the composition of this cross which lies before us, and which Christ bids us bear. There are *convictions* in that cross. Conviction means to "be conquered with." Before we can follow Christ we must be conquered with the belief that He is right, and that His way is right for the world. And then we have to live it! A day would come when the apostles would have to say, "We must obey God rather than men,"[12] and to suffer for their convictions. Someone has spoken of the "risk of belief" and it is indeed a risk. There is a peril in convictions, a peril as real as a cross.

When the Church becomes a place of cushioned ease where men seek only for peace, rather than a place where Christ stands with a cross, then the Church has taken one way and her Master has taken another. But someone will cry: This is too hard and demanding. And then there will come that whine: "A man must live."

> "A man must live! We justify
> Low shift and trick, to treason high;
> A little vote for a little gold,
> Or a whole Senate bought and sold,
> With this self-evident reply—
> 'A man must live!'
>
> "But is it so? Pray tell me why
> Life at such cost you have to buy.
> In what religion were you told
> A man must live?
> There are times when a man must die!
> There are times when a man will die!
> Imagine for a battle-cry
> From soldiers with a sword to hold,
> From soldiers with a flag unfurled,
> This coward's whine, this liar's lie,
> 'A man must live!' "[13]

Need it be added that the Saviour did not live?

The Abbé d'Ars said that in the Middle Ages the greatest fear was the fear of crosses. This is the fear of the twentieth century. Yet the central symbol of Christianity is a cross—not a sleeping pill or a tranquilizer. The story of Anton Lang and the tourist is worth repeating many times. Mr. Lang used to play the Christus in the passion play at Oberammergau. After one performance a tourist decided to have a picture taken of himself bearing the cross used in the play. To his amazement, the cross was so heavy that he was unable to lift it, except with great difficulty. When Mr. Lang appeared, the tourist turned to him in great astonishment and inquired why such a heavy cross must be used in the play. Why not a lighter cross? And Lang replied: "If I could not feel the weight of His cross, I could not play His part." One hymn has it that when we get to heaven, we shall "cast our crowns before Him."[14] It will be better to cast our crosses before Him who bore His own for us.

THE UNANSWERABLE QUESTION

"For whoever would save his life will lose it, and whoever loses his life for my sake will find it. For what will it profit a man, if he gains the whole world and forfeits his life?"[15] Jesus here raises the stakes to their very highest limit—the living soul. We are not playing games and toying with words. There is a deadly seriousness about this matter of bearing the cross—as serious as the loss of the soul. "What shall a man give in return for his life?"[16] This is the unanswerable question.

Just as some marriages are dead and continue in name only, so there are some people who are already dead even though they apparently live. Something vital can die in a man seeking to save himself from discomfort and inconvenience, from sacrifice and distress. Faith becomes foolishness. Mercy and charity go a-begging. Love and generosity of spirit is for fools. Faith is for children. Let the church take its place, providing there is no real inconvenience. Let Christ and His cross keep at a distance.

In this miserliness of spirit, it is possible to reach a more horrible point—a point where that part of us that lives forever is lost. We speak of losing the soul and cannot begin to imagine what that means. In seeking to save, we can be lost. In seeking to preserve we can be left with nothing but rust and corruption. What does it profit a man if he is listed in Dunn and Bradstreet, educated to the hilt, poised and confident in any situation—perhaps even mentioned as a man of distinction—but if with it all he loses his own soul? No one has yet answered our Lord's uncomfortable and piercing question.

THE GREATEST ADVENTURE

But the fact that countless numbers of men and women have deliberately picked up their crosses and followed Christ would indicate that though the cost is great, the reward is even greater. It is still the most wonderful adventure in the world. Those who emerge from the Jordan are clean; and there is a bright word here: "Whoever loses his life for my sake will find it."[17] In following Christ nothing really good is flung away. A man finds himself, and the best part of himself at that, in the train of the Galilean.

"If any man would come after me"—and that in itself ought to be enough. It is Christ we are called to follow. It is Christ who stands with a cross. The Great Antagonist who meets us upon the level of our faith is none other than He. We are called to give ourselves in eternal fealty to Him—and His authority encompasses heaven and earth. His presence is unfailing, and His companionship is both living water and living bread. There is a higher homage than dollars, power, votes, or social prestige. And we shall not begin to do what we ought to do in the world until we find that homage.

To follow Jesus Christ—even with a cross—is still the most wonderful adventure in the world. It is

"To thrill with the joy of girded men,
To go on forever, and fail and go on again . . ."[18]

The tragedy of Judas was the adventure he flung away for thirty pieces of silver. Jesus looks at us with loving trust, after He has given us unflinchingly the cost of coming after Him, and says: "I am sure you will come: you are too big to keep out of it!"[19] The world is poor exchange indeed compared with following Him and one day standing in His Father's house and seeing Him come toward us; and before we can begin to be ashamed of our failures or proud of our scars, to hear Him say: "Well done . . . Well done."

CHAPTER VIII

The Triune Discipline

"My spirit bare before Thee stands;
I bring no gift, I ask no sign,
I come to Thee with empty hands,
The surer to be filled from Thine."

DORA GREENWELL[1]

THERE are three fundamental disciplines of the Christian Faith that cannot be ignored, except at peril of a sterile faith and a sterile spiritual life. They are not spectacular, and they have formed the theme of many a pulpit exhortation. They remain fundamental. They are the triune disciplines of prayer, worship, and the reading of the Holy Bible.

Although these may be done separately, they are inseparable. There is worship in prayer and prayer in worship. There is worship in reading the Bible and reading the Bible is part of worship. And the Bible to be rightly read must be read with prayer.

But are these indeed disciplines? Are they not rather the concomitants of a sentimental picture of an aged mother in a comfortable chair comforting herself in her latter years? So perhaps a sophisticated age has pictured it—and has relegated prayer, worship, and Bible study to the place of lavender and old lace.

THE DISCIPLINE OF THE WORD

The Bible refuses to remain in the corner. One of the most amazing facts of history is the the persistence of the Bible. Its collection of writings spans nearly three millennia. It has recorded the rise and fall of great nations and great men. It has been translated and retranslated—copied and recopied. It has endured the upheavals of history and the not always sympathetic examination of critics. In spite of enemies that have attempted its destruction, the Bible remains. The Bible remains, even when its friends through overweening friendship have shackled it with chains it was never meant to bear. Radical naturalism has attempted to explain away the Bible. Humanistic liberalism has attempted to liberalize its great and piercing truths, and to bring the God of the Bible down to the level of man. Still others have attempted to fix the Bible with "theories" about its inspiration; but in doing so they have sometimes forced the Bible to drag chains which have hampered its message.

In spite of these and many other things, the Bible continues—with an amazing kind of dogged persistence. It is still the world's best seller. The man who has not paid serious attention to his Bible in a long time might well ask, Why? The Bible does not endure because it is printed on expensive paper with gold leaf edges and bound in funeral black. The Bible does not endure because of any theory about its inspiration. It endures and persists for the simple and undramatic reason that it speaks truth.

What kind of truth does the Bible speak? Here is a new generation seeking guidance for life and the living of life: With simple dignity the Bible speaks truth to that generation: "Thou shalt not steal. Thou shalt not bear false witness against thy neighbour. . . . Thou shalt love the Lord thy God with all thy heart . . . Thou shalt love thy neighbour as thyself. . . . Blessed are the pure in heart . . . Blessed are the peacemakers . . . Blessed are the merciful."[2] These old words need no theory for their upstanding. They speak truth. They call to mind the things that are right and the things that are wrong. They tell each generation what is needed if it is to learn to live wisely and justly upon the earth.

Here is a man or woman capable of great deeds. To them the Bible speaks: "If ye have faith as a grain of mustard seed, ye shall say unto this mountain, Remove hence to yonder place; and it shall remove; and nothing shall be impossible unto you."[3] To generation after generation, the Bible has spoken of the dignity and worth of the individual in the sight of God. The Bible has reminded us that we are a little lower than the angels, and have been given dominion over the fowl of the air and the fish of the sea. (All anglers will rejoice in this!) The Bible speaks of the divinely implanted possibilities of human personality and calls man to take the earth in his hands and conquer it—discover its secrets—and walk as a king upon it.

Here also is a man stained by sin. He stands before this ancient word of healing: "If we confess our sins, he is faithful and just to forgive us our sins, and to cleanse us from all unrighteousness." . . . "For God sent the Son into the world, not to condemn the world, but that the world might be saved through him."[4] Before this word, he feels as Christian felt in *Pilgrim's Progress,* when he came in sight of the cross and the burden rolled off his back.

Here is a soul sore beset by life, and desperately in need of help. There is a rock-like strength in the Bible. There is the sanctuary of the Twenty-third Psalm, the Cathedral of the Skies in John 14. There are many quiet chapels in the Bible where one may enter and find rest. There is a peace which the world cannot give and which the world cannot take away.

Yet in spite of all this—and in spite of its continued sale—the Bible is not read today. This is not a philippic against non-readers of the Bible, but the fact remains. People read books about the Bible but they do not read the Bible. The Bible is revered—but it is not read. Yet a part of the discipline of the Christian Faith is the discipline of reading the Bible.

The Bible must be read with *help*. Let us face this. The

layman needs help in understanding many parts of the Bible. He needs historical background, for example. He needs instruction in the literature of the Bible. What is an apocalypse? What was the historical background of the writing of the book of Daniel? This help can be found in two places primarily. First, it can be found in certain books about the Bible such as Bible dictionaries and encyclopedias. Second, this help can be found in a teaching pulpit. One of the main functions of the ministry is to teach. This means, of course, that the ministry must fulfill its function of teaching; and the people must enable the ministry to fulfill that function—by coming to hear the instruction, and by allowing the minister time to prepare. If there is to be a general return to a reading of the Bible, it will not be done without the discipline of study.

Understanding is dependent upon the reading of the whole Bible. A verse here and there, selected at random, is not really reading the Bible. More often than not, it is using the Bible as some kind of talisman or fetish. The Bible must be read as a Book and as individual books, and each part must speak in its context. Many people have repeated, "If God be for us, who can be against us?"[5] and have no idea of the gallant context from which it comes, nor of the realities of the life out of which it speaks.

This is a frank plea for a lay return to studying the Bible under competent instruction and with much personal prayer. There is already strong indication of a clerical return to teaching and preaching the Bible. In many instances, however, weaknesses in the witness of the Church and of individual Christians, theological controversies between laymen and clergy, as well as the increase of nominal church members, may be traced to an ignorance of the teachings of the Bible as well as of the doctrines of the Christian Faith which spring from the Bible. Even the so-called "Bible belt" in the South is seeing a growing Biblical illiteracy.

The reading of the Bible is a discipline. It requires first

the discipline of *time*. This is simply said, but not so simply followed. Time is our master today and we are the slaves. If the Bible is read at all, it is usually read in snatches—a verse here or there after a tiring day, when our thoughts are primarily on sleep. God has always had difficulty in speaking to a sleepy man—ever since the days of Samuel![6] No wonder the prophets were continually calling upon people to awake out of their sleep. Time that is fresh and of some length must be set aside for the Bible—possibly at the expense of a favorite television program.

The Bible requires also the discipline of *prayer and devotion*. The Bible must be loved to be understood. And those who have truly devoted themselves to the Bible have loved it not because the Bible is considered some kind of fetish, but because they have loved the truth of God they have found there. Hence real prayer is a concomitant to reading the Bible. True reading of the Bible is also true prayer; for in the Bible we can hold converse with God. As He spoke to Abraham, Moses, Isaiah, and Paul, He can speak again through them to us. The travails of the psalmist are not so far removed from us; and we walk with the psalmist a mutual path to the throne of God's mercy and help. An account of the crucifixion cannot be read without a prayer. The Holy Spirit of God is not limited. As we read and pray, He will lead us into truth.

There is something else that needs to be said: The Bible requires the discipline of *action*. The Bible was not written to be contemplated for itself alone. This is the present danger of the return to Biblical preaching, as well as of the present general emphasis upon the Bible. The Bible may become an end in itself, rather than a means to an end.

The Bible was struck off in life—and is meant to be carried into life. Abraham left a flesh-and-blood civilization of comfort, and if archaeology be correct, with a culture comparable to our own. He sacrificed something real for his faith. Paul put everything that mattered in a material way behind him because of Christ. The prophets were battling real sins of profiteering, loose living, and injustice of all kinds. The New Testament Church faced real lions, rather than deny their Lord. And the Roman Empire was most earnestly determined to destroy this new religion that threatened its very existence.

Our times are no less real. For this reason, a real study of the Bible is no less dangerous. For the Bible still calls for committal. There are "orders" in the Bible—strong compelling words: "Go, preach, give, love, deny, serve." There are words that challenge prejudices: "If your enemy is hungry, feed him." . . . "Love . . . your neighbor as yourself."[7] The Bible calls us not only to clasp our hands above, but also to spread them abroad in service. The voice of God in the Bible may be still and small, but it is not the less compelling.

In this connection, the reading of the Bible calls for the discipline of a *constant repentance*. The quarrelsome are judged by this: "Blessed are the peacemakers."[8] The dark and impure cannot stand before this: "Blessed are the pure in heart."[9] This is a judgment upon the stingy: "Give . . . good measure, pressed down . . . running over . . ."[10] And the critical must listen to this: "Why do you see the speck that is in your brother's eye, but do not notice the log that is in your own eye?"[11]

The Bible is an amazing mirror. It speaks out of the ages to the ages. In the Bible every man can see himself.

"Stone crumbles, but more staunchly fares
A dust incredibly translated:
Judas still haggles at his wares,
Cain is forever new created.
Delilah in a Paris frock
Goes out to tea at five o'clock;
Salome climbs the subway stairs,
Potiphar takes the elevated."[12]

"A dust incredibly translated"—look around and you will see another Abraham looking for something better, looking for a City which has foundations. Here is a Joseph who trusted God and overcame his circumstances. The rich young ruler still turns back to his gold and position. The woman taken in adultery is still flung at the feet of a compassionate Christ. There is the undying devotion of a woman breaking the alabaster jar. Faithful women at the tomb still keep faithful vigil, even though they fear that Truth is dead. There is still an Amos of social conscience. Sennacherib is revived in every dictator. The lost sheep are in every crowd. Judas still sells his Lord and Peter dies for Him. People are still sitting down by the waters of Babylon or the Danube and weeping because the Lord's song is dim in their hearts.

The Bible is the tears and the laughter, the black and the white and the gray of man. But in it there is a gentle Voice and a commanding eye: "I am the good shepherd . . . the resurrection and the life . . . If any man would come after me, let him deny himself and take up his cross and follow me. . . . Peace I leave with you."[13] The discipline of reading the Bible reveals not only ourselves but Jesus Christ.

THE DISCIPLINE OF WORSHIP

Worship is almost a lost word in our time. It either calls to mind a ritual that no one understands, or a duty to attend church when one would rather be somewhere else. But worship is neither ritual nor church attendance alone. From the days of the prophets until now, worship is not "temple trampling" nor a routine going to church on a Sunday morning.

The discipline of worship is first of all a *humility*. It is a bowing-before Someone greater—a prostration of the spirit in adoration: "O come, let us worship and bow down; let us kneel before the Lord our maker."[14] "I saw the Lord," said Isaiah, "high and lifted up."[15] The old proverb has it that the mountain shames the molehill until both are shamed by the stars. Worship is first standing beneath eternal stars. Worship is seeing an eternal Throne and knowing that kingdoms rise and fall but one Kingdom remains.

There is also *confession* in the discipline of worship. Someone greater is also Someone holier. Worship is not worship unless it creates a shame and a desire for cleansing: "Create in me a clean heart, O God,"[16] is the prayer of a man at the business of true worship. "I am a man of unclean lips," cried Isaiah in the Temple.[17] He was at worship—when he saw God and he saw himself.

Again, there is *dedication* in the discipline of worship. If we can turn from a house of worship and not have heard a single command, not have felt a single desire to amend our ways and our doings, then we have not really worshiped. After Isaiah had had his tremendous experience of worship in the Temple, his response was, "Here I am! Send me."[18] Worship ought to result in the feeling of being "sent." It ought to bring us to a Person of commanding eye and gentle heart who calls us to follow Him. "The worship is over," said an usher to a latecomer, "but," he added with unconscious insight, "the *service* is just beginning."

Too much of Protestant worship today is a spectator kind of worship. In our haste to avoid the presumable taint of liturgy, we have thrown out the baby with the bath. Too often the average Protestant congregation sits back and waits to be "entertained," exhorted, or otherwise kept reasonably occupied for an hour. Worship has become a word and not an act.

All this is not to discount preaching. "It pleased God by the foolishness of preaching to save them that believe," said Paul.[19] The doctrine of the Christian pulpit has always been an unwritten doctrine of the Christian Church. From the very beginning, preaching has had a central place. In the sermon, Christ crucified is lifted up; and there should take place a kind of "communion through preaching."[20] The sermon should be an act of worship in itself. Needless to say, this is a terrible responsibility—to know that you the preacher are the only person between your people and the worship of Jesus Christ! David Hume, that dour Scots philosopher, apparently had little praise for any preacher. Yet he had it for one man at least, for of that man he wrote: "He preaches as though Jesus Christ were at his elbow." So there is a discipline for the one who leads the worship as well as for the worshiper.

The writer cannot resist making a plea here on behalf of the preacher. Arthur John Gossip has written in his splendid way of the tremendous conception of the sermon in Reformed worship. He writes that the preacher comes out to the pulpit "from the hush and secret of the Presence, where for a week he has been listening and brooding, face to face with God in a silence other men cannot attain, and where the divine voice can carry clearly."[21] This is a wonderful statement—but the plain truth is that the preacher does *not* have a week to listen! And the word "hush" is a far cry from the hubbub of modern life, the stringent tension of the hospital, the person in agony of soul. This no man with a pastor's heart will neglect. Yet it means that his hours to prepare are precious and few, in comparison to the task he faces on Sunday. He must have *time*—if he is to do what great Reformed worship calls him to do on Sunday morning.

The preacher must also be *free,* if he is to do what Protestant worship calls him to do. In the last days of the judges of Israel, when every man did that which was right in his own eyes, we read in First Samuel a frightening commentary on the times: "And the word of the Lord was precious in those days; there was *no open vision.*"[22] If we shackle the pulpit and require from the preacher only that which is palatable to our ears, we are in danger of coming again to the point where the word of the Lord will be rare and there will be no open vision. The shackling of the Protestant pulpit can be the most dangerous thing that can happen to freedom. The people must not say again to the preachers as they did in the days of Isaiah: "Speak to us smooth things, prophesy illusions."[23] For then it will come to pass, as John Bunyan declared in *Pilgrim's Progress,* "I saw that there was a way to hell, even from the gates of heaven."[24]

"To save them that believe"—here we have to do with something that has eternal proportions. Worship for preacher and congregation is no idle matter of passing a dutiful hour on Sunday morning. The preacher does not stand in a place of academic interest. He stands between Heaven and Hell, and his people stand with him. He stands there because God in His wisdom chose to put him there. Let him stand, splendidly unchained except by the love of his Christ. For there he must stand, and bravely proclaim that Jesus is Lord, until God takes the trumpet from his lips.

THE DISCIPLINE OF PRAYER

Jesus once said that men "ought always to pray and not lose heart."[25] The times that He spent apart in prayer are shining examples. If He, the Master, should pray, the disciple can do no less. Prayer is the fundamental Christian discipline. These paragraphs about prayer are not intended to be exhaustive, only indicative. There are many excellent books on Christian prayer.

First of all, prayer is *praise.* Prayer's first concern is with the greatness and holiness of the Creator and not the creature. The discipline of great prayer is to pray first that the Father's Name be hallowed and that His Kingdom come. We have already said that the discipline of worship is humility—a bowing before Someone greater. This is also true of prayer. Great worship, as well as great prayer, is begun by the prayer of praise and humility. This is discipline because it means that we must first acknowledge that God—and not man—is the center of the universe.

To see the King is to see ourselves—and it is not always a pretty sight. Isaiah's "Woe is me" was wrung from a man who had seen the King. Hence the second discipline of prayer, as in worship, is *confession*. Someone will cry "morbid." It is indeed morbid to dwell upon our sins until we are despairing, or, worse, until that dwelling becomes a subtle pleasure. But it is not morbid to confess; rather, it is therapy. And let it be said also that confession is not to confess to the Divine Executive, "I have not been a success today"! Rather Christian confession is to acknowledge to the Father in heaven that "against thee, thee only, have I sinned."[26] If sin does not stand like a specter over our prayers, then we have not truly prayed—or worshiped.

Prayer is also *dedication*. Before a prayer is ended there ought to be a "Here I am! Send me."[27] The discipline of dedication is not easy. Our first thought is to look for what God can do for us, rather than what we can do for God. Prayer is gauged as being successful if we are successful in getting what we want from God. But Jesus taught us to pray for the Father's will to be done and for His Kingdom to come. Prayer is not a battle of wills, but a submission of will to God. Even our Lord in Gethsemane prayed for the Father's will to be done. The disciple is not greater than his Master. Prayer that attempts to dictate to the Almighty is verging upon blasphemy. Prayer that does not cry, even in sweat like drops of blood, for the divine will to be done is not Christian.

Prayer is *petition,* but petition that is discipline. Jesus taught His followers to pray for their daily bread. The human impulse is to pray for tomorrow's bread also—and possibly even bread for the day after that! We are prone, too, to ask for more than bread. Jesus said that the Father knows what things we have need of before we ask Him.[28] We are inclined to want to jog His memory. It is not wrong to make material requests of God; but we ought to discipline ourselves severely in the making of those requests. There may be some value in praying that we shall make that important sale tomorrow—but we shall do better on that sale if we let prayer cleanse us first that we may be in a better frame of mind when we approach the prospect. It is not wrong to pray that we pass the examination, but it is wrong to ask God to bless the efforts of a lazy mind.

Prayer is not always answered according to our desires. "The patience of unanswered prayer" is one of prayer's disciplines.[29] If the answers to prayer be a gauge of prayer's success, then most Christians would have to say that their prayers are unsuccessful. Successful prayer is cleansing; it is the redirection of the will and a mind fixed upon God. It is not bearing away things from the throne of grace, as one would carry groceries from a market place.

Hence Christian prayer is not a posture but a state of mind. It is not a condition of the body but a condition of the soul. In this sense, the Christian can indeed pray without ceasing as Paul enjoined him to do. But we do not arrive at this condition overnight. Successful Christian prayer comes out of the discipline and practice of the years. It comes from the discipline of daily living in the sight of God's burning holiness and His Fatherly concern.

These three disciplines are indivisible. The Bible, prayer, and worship cannot be separated from one another. There is worship in prayer and prayer in worship. There is worship in reading the Bible and reading the Bible is a part of worship. And the Bible to be rightly read must be read with prayer.

The alternative to these disciplines of the Christian religion is a sterile faith—an intellectual assent only. The result of these disciplines is peace of mind and stability of soul. Those who practice them do not "faint" at life and the business of living. They stand when others have fallen.

Ours is an age that is re-examining religion. A re-examination of the Christian religion will sooner or later reveal its strong disciplines to be standing like sentinels along the way to the City of God.

"Thy will be done, on earth as it is in heaven."
Matthew 6:10

PART THREE

THE STRONG COMMAND

"There may be heaven; there must be hell;
Meantime, there is our earth here—well!"
ROBERT BROWNING
"Time's Revenges"

CHAPTER IX

A Time Out of Joint

"The time is out of joint;—O cursed spite,
That ever I was born to set it right."

WILLIAM SHAKESPEARE[1]

THERE have been Hamlets in every age who have cried that the time is out of joint. There is Cicero crying in the Roman Senate: "O tempora, O mores!" In the 1500's, the French philosopher Montaigne wrote: "The age we live in is so dull and leaden that not only the execution but the very imagination of virtue is far to seek." In the 1600's, John Tillotson the historian and Archbishop of Canterbury wrote: "Men have hardened their faces in this degenerate age." And in our time there are plenty who are ready to write this age off in an atomic cloud.

It is true that our times are out of joint. For all the revival of interest in religion, ours is still a secular age. Dr. Georgia Harkness rightly calls secularism "The foremost rival of Christianity." Secular means life organized with God left out, and life is pretty much organized that way. To many the Church is still a social convenience, not a necessity. Christ is revered but not followed. Prayer is a crutch, not a driving power. The Bible is not really known. Men feel that money, time, and abilities belong to them alone, to do with as they please. They live as though their books were never to receive the eye of a Divine Auditor.

The national and international scene is also a scene "out of joint." We are in a time of vexed human relations, when good and sincere men are in a quandary about where to turn. The bombing of churches and homes is but a symptom of a deeper sickness. No one knows where the next crisis will focus international discord. Civil defense remains an uncomfortable thought, and we try to forget the sign along the well-kept highway: "In the event of enemy attack, this highway may be closed . . ."

"IN MY HEART AS . . . A BURNING FIRE"

One thing is certain. We are held to our time. We cannot escape either forward or backward. It is useless to curse the day. It is better to believe that we were born to put it right. This is the strong command of the Christian Faith.

When an age curses itself, and can find no solution to its dilemma, it is at a desperate juncture. When a man curses the day he was born he also is at a desperate juncture. The twentieth chapter of Jeremiah is a soliloquy from the depths and the story of a man who cursed his time. Pashur, head of the Temple police and corresponding to a Gestapo chieftain or secret police of today, has arrested Jeremiah and put him in the stocks at the Temple entrance.

In his desperate dilemma Jeremiah curses his time: "Cursed be the day wherein I was born."[2] His nation hastens to a self-chosen path to doom; and his reward for warning them is persecution, ridicule, and now the cruel stocks. So the man lifts up his great head and curses his time:

> "Why did I come forth from the womb
> to see toil and sorrow,
> and spend my days in shame?"[3]

In his bitterness, Jeremiah determines that he will speak for God no longer, that he will shut his mouth and his spirit, withdraw completely, and renounce his prophetic office. For a prophet of God this is the ultimate denunciation:

> ". . . I will not mention him,
> or speak any more in his name."[4]

The words lie like tears over a face resigned.

Yet even in the depths Jeremiah is held to his place:

> "There is in my heart as it were a burning fire
> shut up in my bones,
> and I am weary with holding it in,
> and I cannot."[5]

It is true that Jeremiah did not save his nation from doom. Yet by proclaiming the truth of a God of love and justice he preserved a remnant who believed and carried the faith back from exile. He sowed a good seed that later bore fruit. *He spoke a clear word in a confused time and set the record straight, even if men did not choose to follow it.* He was one of God's "saving" men and women.

We are just as much held to our time as was Jeremiah. Escape forward or backward, and we shall only exchange our pains. Some are tempted to give way and cry "doom," cover their heads and wait for the end. But while Cicero was crying doom in the Roman Senate, Christ was coming to be born at Bethlehem. Tillotson cried, "Degenerate age," but that was also the age of John Bunyan and George Fox. Montaigne saw no virtue in his age, but he was contemporary with Martin Luther. An English revolution similar to the one in France was prevented in no little measure by the preaching of a man named John Wesley.

The Christian Faith hurls its people against their time as God hurled Jeremiah against his time, as Jesus sent eleven men into the decadent Roman Empire. The Christian Faith calls for "saving" men and women who are witnesses to God's truth in word and life; who will be sowers of good seed for a future year; who will stand in home, church, government, and business and write a straight record before God and man.

Our times may be out of joint, but it will do no good to curse them or to curse the fact that we live in them. Every man must look to his own house, to his own armor and sword.

The times are indeed "nightfall," as Gerard Manley Hopkins reminds us; and then stabs with a greater truth:

> "The times are nightfall, look, their light grows less;
> The times are winter, watch, a world undone:
>
> . . . .
>
> Or what is else? There is your world within.
> There rid the dragons, root out there the sin."[6]

"Cursed be the day"—aye, curse the day if we must. But that will not light a single candle; that will not right a single wrong. Cry that God has deceived and that we will not speak any more in His name; but that will not stir a single planet from its place in the majestic universe. Say rather: "His Word of truth, His great act of redeeming love in Christ, is in my heart as a burning fire, and I cannot hold it in. Regardless of the times, I shall give my hand and heart to Him. I shall have my part in the obedience of the wheeling stars."

"A MAN TO STAND IN THE GAP"

God looks in every age for men who will "stand in the gap." In the year 599 Babylon invaded Judah and laid siege to Jerusalem. In that year the great battering rams of the Babylonian army succeeded in making a breach in the wall of Jerusalem. The invaders poured through and carried the people captive. Later, in retrospect, the prophet Ezekiel spoke for God: "And I sought for a man among them, that should make up the hedge, *and stand in the gap* before me for the land, that I should not destroy it: but I found none."[7]

A close reading of Ezekiel 22 will reveal that there were breached walls in every facet of the nation's society—government, home, and church. God had been looking for men who would stand in the gaps. The breach made by Babylon's armies was not as great as the gaps Judah's people had already opened in their nation by their lives.

God looks for men today who will stand in the gap. God looks for men and women who by their moral and spiritual fiber and sinew will be able to stand in the breached gaps and build up the wall before Him.

In Ezekiel's day, the princes destroyed lives "to get dishonest gain."[8] The priests made "no distinction between the holy and the common."[9] The Sabbaths were disregarded. Like leaders, like people; the "people of the land . . . practiced extortion and committed robbery; they . . . oppressed the poor and needy."[10] We are not so comfortably removed from these sins as we would like to think.

But perhaps worst of all, the "prophets . . . daubed for them with whitewash, seeing false visions and divining lies for them, saying, 'Thus says the Lord God,' when the Lord has not spoken."[11] The preachers would not tell the people the truth. They compromised, and whitewashed their sermons. No doubt they were under extreme pressure to do so. Their jobs were at stake. But they forgot that the life of a nation and a people was also at stake. There can be breached walls in the pulpit as well as in government, the home, and business.

A nation is at stake. An age is at stake: "That I should not destroy it,"[12] said God. Nations have been destroyed. Whole ages have lain in ruins, when the vessel would not shape to the will of the Potter. A Divine Teacher has written His lessons large in history. He looks for men to stand in the gap. In times past, He found Peter, James, and John. A little man named Paul was hurled into the gaps of the Roman Empire. Luther was cast into the breach of a Church that needed reforming. Today an age and a world are at stake. And God looks for men.

"THE CHARIOTS OF ISRAEL"

Our age will not be saved with swords, but with ideas and the men who embody them. There are chariots in thoughts and horsemen in ideas. The history of the world is the story of powerful ideas and thoughts. Moses went down into Egypt with the idea of one God of justice and withstood the power of Egypt. It was the idea of Christianity that helped bring down the Roman Empire. Ghandi's idea of passive resistance confounded Britain. We all know the saying: "Mightier than an army is the power of an idea whose time has come."[13]

An idea does not have to be good or bad to "find terrifying lodgment in a historical situation." Witness the idea of Communism. Jesus recognized this when He warned: "What comes out of a man is what defiles a man."[14] And out of the heart come lying, murder, adultery. That which comes out of men's thinking can be most terrible. In our own time, what men think is becoming tremendously important. G. K. Chesterton was not so far wrong when he once suggested that a landlady should first inquire of a lodger what is his philosophy of life!

When Elisha, the prophet of God, lay on his deathbed, Joash, king of Israel, came to see him and wept over him: "My father, my father! The chariots of Israel and its horsemen!"[15] It is a thought-provoking picture. Joash is a man in full vigor. Outside are his chariots and retainers—an army to command. Elisha is a dying old man whose strength is almost gone—a man who had never wielded a sword or commanded a battalion. And Joash weeps over him as "the chariots of Israel." For a moment in his life, Joash grasped real truth—the truth that moral force is greater than physical force—that ideas are more powerful than bullets.

Part of the strength of a nation consists in the ideas behind it. The ideas behind the United States, for example, are justice, general welfare, and the blessings of liberty. The Constitution speaks of freedom of religion, freedom of speech, freedom of the press. One of its great ideas is "rights"—the right of private property, the right of trial. These great ideas have helped mold the nation and have been her "chariots and horsemen." Our armies might be defeated, but these ideas are trampled upon at great danger to the national fiber. A building torn down may be rebuilt; but an idea destroyed is much harder to rebuild. And the greatest strength of the nation lies still in the great ideas resident in the Church and Gospel of Jesus Christ. These are still "the chariots of Israel and the horsemen thereof."

Ideas and words embodied in men created the Christian Church. Jesus Christ never wrote a book or drafted a written charter for His Church. The first Christian apostles went out with literally nothing in their hands—carrying neither script nor purse and saluting no man by the way. There was no visible army with them when they first entered a village or city. But before a man like Paul had left a place, the town knew that a force not of this world had been there.

The story of Christianity is still one of the most amazing stories of history—the story of ordinary men and a carpenter from Nazareth who was executed by the Romans in an obscure province named Judea. The pagans laughed at first, but it was not long before they were thrusting these people into the flames and the mouths of lions in a desperate attempt to burn out this terrible Idea that was riding through the Roman Empire like an invincible chariot of war. They might tear down the church on the corner, looking for that power that lifts empires off their hinges, but they would not find it. They must turn to men who bear these ideas in their hearts like burning fires.

Resident in the Christian Faith are great words and great ideas: Justice, Love, Charity, Freedom, and the Dignity of the Individual; Prayer, Repentance, Faith, Salvation, Service. There is the impulse to charity: "Love one another."[16] There is the missionary impulse: "Make disciples of all nations."[17] The idea of sacrificial service is here: "Let him . . . take up his cross."[18] There are the great healing ideas of salvation and forgiveness: "If we confess our sins, he is faithful and just, and will forgive . . ."[19] These are the "chariots of Israel." And they are resident in men, not in buildings.

The real strength of the age will not be in guided missiles and gadgets for comfort, but in people who are sworn to

Christ, who live mercy, truth, and justice daily. These are "the Lord's arrow of victory."[20] These are the people whose faith has lived "in spite of dungeon, fire, and sword."[21] They have been civilization's rear guard against death and disease, evil and injustice. The sound of their treading upon the earth is the sound of a mighty army. God is looking for men who will be "the chariots of Israel."

FAITH BEYOND OUR TIME

To speak of our times as "out of joint" is to put it mildly. Extreme pessimism is more the order of the day. There is need for gallantry and optimism. Rufus Jones tells of climbing high in the Swiss Alps and finding near the top a monument with these words: "*Das Enderwelt*"—the end of the world. But, pushing on a little farther, he discovered that the trail did not really end there but led beyond. So the men who stand in the gaps today must believe that in spite of the darkness of the times, the trail does lead beyond. They must have faith beyond their time.

One of the Bible's most gallant scenes is that of Jeremiah buying the field of Anathoth. He is shut up in prison and his people believe him a traitor. Nebuchadnezzar's army is besieging Jerusalem, and the fall of the city and the nation is imminent.

> "A voice is heard in Ramah,
> lamentation and bitter weeping.
> Rachel is weeping for her children."[22]

It would have appeared that this was "Das Enderwelt" for Jeremiah and his time. Into his cell comes a visitor, his cousin Hanamel, with an almost ridiculous request. He asks Jeremiah to buy back a field near Anathoth—a piece of property that had been in Jeremiah's family for generations. The request was in accordance with Hebrew law. If a member of the family saw that he was about to lose some of his land, then he must try to get some other member of the family to redeem it. But the idea now was ridiculous—buy land trampled by the boot of the invader!

To the astonishment of everyone, Jeremiah calls for witnesses, a scribe, and scales to weigh the money. Then, with Nebuchadnezzar's siege machinery sounding dully within the walls of the prison, with the shouts of soldiers heard on the walls, the money is weighed and the deed signed. Jeremiah pushes around "Das Enderwelt" and looks beyond his time: "For thus says the Lord of hosts, the God of Israel: Houses and fields and vineyards shall again be bought in this land."[23]

Here was a gallant word of hope when there appeared to be no hope. Jeremiah's cell became a chapel, like Paul's cell in Rome and Bunyan's cell in Newgate Prison. "Jesus Christ came into my cell last night," said James Guthrie the Covenanter, "and every stone shone like a ruby." "He has delivered us," said Paul, "from the dominion of darkness."[24] Our Lord in His farewell address to His apostles did not spare them what was to come. But then He turned at the door with a happy smile—even upon the threshold of Gethsemane and the cross: "So you have sorrow now, but I will see you again and your hearts will rejoice."[25] This is not "Das Enderwelt." The trail leads beyond.

A national magazine once carried a terrifying article about how the earth came into being and how it would one day possibly be destroyed. The whole thing was accompanied by vividly illustrative drawings. Particularly terrifying was the drawing illustrating how the sun would explode like a huge hydrogen bomb and the earth would melt like butter and be burned to a cinder! But the earth is still "the Lord's, and the fulness thereof."[26] Jeremiah bought a little packet of earth and took courage, because the earth was under God. Paul wrote a few letters and flung them like seed before the wind, believing that the truth they presented would live because it was under God. This *posture of faith* is that to which we are called—the posture of faith that looks beyond our time and hopes in God, even when armies lay siege to the walls.

Archibald Rutledge, in his little book *Life's Extras,* tells of driving his horse and buggy home at night when a terrible storm arose. Lightning split the sky and thunder rolled constantly. Great trees came crashing down along the road. His horse could stand it no longer but broke loose and smashed the buggy against the sides of two trees. Mr. Rutledge was left stranded in the rain and tempest. As he stood there wondering which way to go, he saw a tiny rift in the cloud—and through the rift he saw the evening star. And it seemed to him that the star was saying: "This storm is an impostor. It is momentary. The sky is here, and the stars; all shall be well."[27]

Jeremiah believed Babylon was but an impostor. Paul believed his cell was but an impostor. Jesus believed the cross would pass. The strong command of the Christian Faith is to live under God in a time out of joint. It is a responsible task and calls for men who live the truth and do justly. But at all times it calls for men who will have faith beyond their time—who will believe that the storm is but an impostor, and only God remains.

CHAPTER X

On Earth as It Is in Heaven

> "The most pressing necessity for a Christian man, I mean for one who really believes in Christ, even simply in the salvation of his soul, is that he shall have some good work to do."
>
> RICHARD ROTHE[1]

THE strong command of God is to live in our time. The Christian Faith was not designed for a vacuum, but to make an impact upon every time in which its adherents live. Hence there is a very real sense in which the Gospel of Christ is "social." Indeed the "social" gospel, so-called, was born when Jesus taught His disciples to pray:

> "Thy kingdom come,
> Thy will be done,
> On earth as it is in heaven."[2]

Surely it follows that if we pray for the Rule of God to come and the will of God to be done, then that Rule must come and that will must be done—through us.

Someone will plead here that the Gospel of Christ is an evangelical gospel, concerned with the saving of the souls of men. This is true; but if we remain strictly with this view, then there was no need for Jesus Christ to open His mouth, to touch a single leper or cure a single illness. All He need have done was go silently to the cross and die. But plainly Jesus did not do this. He said: "But I say unto you . . ."[3] By example and by word, He taught His disciples to seek the will of God on earth. His Gospel points the way to heaven, but also the way along which we should walk.

"SHOULD NOT I PITY NINEVEH?"

In considering this whole matter of applying the Christian Faith to life and considering the relevance of that Faith to life, there is a basic question: What kind of God is above us? Is He merely a provincial God, concerned only with our nation, our particular part of the nation, our group, race, or social class? If so, then let us make God in our image and bow down to ourselves. The God of the Bible and of the Christian Faith is not provincial but universal. His concern is for all His creatures. His salvation is for "whosoever will."

This lesson is brought into sharp focus in one of the great little books of the Bible, the book of Jonah. The story is familiar, and debates have been carried on *ad infinitum* concerning the "whale." The real point of the story is often missed; for one must read past the story of the "whale" to the very last verse: "You pity the plant, for which you did not labor, nor did you make it grow, which came into being in a night, and perished in a night. And should not I pity Nineveh, that great city, in which there are more than a hundred and twenty thousand persons who do not know their right hand from their left, and also much cattle?"[4]

Jonah was a little man who worshiped a provincial god. So he became violently angry when God did not destroy Nineveh. The Ninevites were not Jews, and moreover they had been wicked in the extreme. Suppose they do repent, let them be destroyed anyway! So Jonah remonstrated with God. He had preached the destruction of Nineveh. Now let Nineveh be destroyed. But the people of Nineveh repented, and the city was spared.

Believing that God was making a dreadful mistake, Jonah went outside the city and sat down to wait, still hoping for the destruction of Nineveh—a spectacle which promised to be every bit as spectacular as the destruction of Sodom and Gomorrah!

The city was not destroyed. And by that time Jonah was displaying more concern over the loss of his sheltering vine than he had over the condition of the people of Nineveh. So God rebukes him: "Should not I pity Nineveh?" It is a question thrown down from heaven: "Jonah, if you find yourself concerned over this ephemeral vine which grew up in a night and perished in a night, should not God Almighty have pity on a great city? What kind of God, Jonah, do you think I am?" Jonah had a little God and a great contempt for his fellow human beings. Jonah had yet to learn that the God of Israel is the God of the whole earth—not the exclusive property of the Jews—and that He will have mercy upon all who call upon Him.

Nearly three hundred years ago, John Donne said it another way: "No man is an island, entire of itself; every man is a piece of the continent, a part of the main; if a clod be washed away by the sea, Europe is the less, as well as if a promontory were . . . Any man's death diminishes me, because I am involved in mankind; and therefore never send to know for whom the bell tolls; it tolls for thee."[5] When the bell tolled for Nineveh, the bell was tolling for Jonah. Jonah was on more than just a charity preaching mission. He was on a mission that involved his own life and death.

From the soil of this principle grow the roots of brotherhood, tolerance, understanding, and good human relations. The kind of God we worship will determine the way we act toward our fellow human beings. Great religion in the life of a people is one which shows God clearly to be a God of all men. In the present time, one of our most acute problems is the problem of human and race relations. This is one of the areas in which our time is upon the fringes of a world revolution. No section of the nation or the world can escape it. The Christian Faith will speak to this crisis only as it points to its God—a Saviour God too big for human differences, whose mercy is wider and broader than the measure of man's mind. Before Him all men stand in need of a common redemption. This God rises in anger at the sight of any man sitting under his vine and watching for his neighbor to die.

"WHO IS MY NEIGHBOR?"

"But he, desiring to justify himself, said to Jesus, 'And who is my neighbor?' "[6] Here is really the crux of the matter. An enunciation of the principle of loving our neighbors as ourselves is not enough. The immediate human reaction, as in the case of the lawyer who asked Jesus the question, is to attempt to put boundaries around "neighborliness." "Who is my neighbor?" suggests discrimination. So Jesus was asked to draw a boundary.

The air was no doubt filled with tension and hatred. In the crowd around Jesus there were probably all kinds of people—Jews, Greeks, a cynical Roman soldier, and people of other races and nations. To the Jews, Gentiles were "dogs." Laws of mercy in the Old Testament were interpreted as applying only to Jews. The Greeks regarded everyone except themselves as uncultured barbarians. The Romans haughtily considered Roman citizenship the most important thing in the world and looked down their Roman noses at anyone who was not a Roman citizen. Even the twelve apostles at one time had been moved to ask, "Lord, if my brother sin against me, how often shall I forgive him?"[7] So the crowd pressed in close. What answer would Jesus give?

Jesus refused to argue. Here we can take a leaf from His book! He told a story to illustrate His point—the parable of the Good Samaritan—a picture that will hang forever in the art galleries of the human mind. "A man was going down from Jerusalem to Jericho, and he fell among robbers."[8] And the hearers had to nod their heads to one another in understanding. They had all at one time or another traveled the Jericho road and its twenty-one tortuous miles dropping three thousand feet to sea level. They had feared the dangers of that road. Anyone in that crowd could have been that man.

The little story unfolds with simple clarity. The priest and Levite hurry by. (Were there some red-faced priests and Levites in that crowd?) The Samaritan comes and endangers himself to bind up the wounds. The helpless man is taken to a hotel, his bills paid. (We remember, of course, that the Jews have no dealings with the Samaritans.) Then the disarming question: "Which of these three, do you think, proved neighbor to the man . . . ?" The answer is obvious: "The one who showed mercy . . ." The strong command comes quietly: "Go and do likewise."[9]

Now the objections and questions begin to press in: Lord, you did not answer the man's question. You did not give him a solution to the problem of Greek, Jew, Roman, and Samaritan. What laws would you enact? What resolutions would you pass?

Jesus did not answer the lawyer's question. It did not deserve an answer; for it is a question akin to the question of Cain: "Am I my brother's keeper?"[10] That question was never answered either except in the awful voice of God: "Your brother's blood is crying to me from the ground."[11] To ask, "Who is my neighbor?" is an attempt to put boundaries around love and mercy and justice, and Jesus Christ steadfastly refused to do that.

Instead, Jesus in this story asked a question far more penetrating and soul-searching: Are you a neighbor? With stern simplicity Jesus does not say whether the man by the road is Jew, Samaritan, Roman, or Greek. The man is identified in only two ways—his need and his humanity. There, said Jesus, is your neighbor.

Suppose we were to run up to Jesus and say, "Lord, tell us about this matter of race relations?" Would not Jesus do what He so often did with such questions—answer the questioner and not the question? The real question is: What do we think about our neighbors, regardless of color, whom we see every day? Then Jesus would lay His hand upon these great words—Justice and Love and Mercy.

This is part of the strong command of the Christian Faith to us who are called to live in our time: Can I be tolerant of the non-Protestant in my own community? Can I treat the man of another race as a human being in my own town? Can I treat with kindness the Jew with whom I do business? Can I forgive my next-door neighbor? Can I learn to love people? And let it be admitted that people are not always easy to love. But, "if you love those who love you, what reward have you? Do not even the tax collectors do the same?"[12] It is always easier to talk in theoretical terms about segregation and discrimination than it is this larger thing of Mercy that searches the soul.

The Samaritan saw the man as a human being and went and helped him. He did not theorize that he was not responsible, that he would go and protest to the authorities about the whole situation on the Jericho road. Suppose the man were a Jew—he did not lump the man in a class who hated him, and so let him lie. He simply went and helped him.

Walt Whitman once wrote these words that are very near the truth to which Jesus was pointing:

> "I do not ask the wounded person how he feels;
> I myself become the wounded person.
> And whoever walks a furlong without sympathy
> Walks to his own funeral drest in his shroud."[13]

Zacchaeus the hated quisling tax collector for the Romans? Ostracize him. The woman of the streets? Stone her. A man of another color? Lump him in a class and quietly forget that he, too, is a human being.

God has long been speaking this strong command to those who would love and serve Him. Long ago, through His prophet Isaiah, He spoke to a people meticulous in their sacrifices and rituals:

"Learn to do good;
seek justice,
correct oppression;
defend the fatherless,
plead for the widow."[14]

"In many and various ways God spoke of old to our fathers by the prophets; but in these last days he has spoken to us by a Son . . ."[15]

Charles Kingsley had this great rule for living: "Make a rule and pray to God to help you keep it—never, if possible, to lie down at night without being able to say: 'I have made one human being at least a little wiser or a little happier or at least a little better this day.' "

The quality of mercy cannot be self-manufactured. It comes only in the realization of God's mercy toward us. The pagan world in the early days of Christianity marveled at the quality of love in the lives of Christians. "How do you do it?" they asked. And John answers simply: "We love, because he first loved us."[16] This, of course, takes us to the cross. Golgotha was the Jericho road, if you will have it. There the Son of God took a cross and ministered to a dying world. There God was taking a broom and sweeping the world for His lost coins. There God was hurrying down the road to greet a prodigal son. So when Paul came to write the great ethical portion of his letter to the Romans, he prefaced it with this reminder: "I appeal to you therefore, brethren, by the mercies of God . . ."[17] Having pointed to the cross, he could then point his people to one another: "Love one another with brotherly affection; outdo one another in showing honor."[18] We only learn to love our neighbors as ourselves, standing at the foot of the cross. There where we pray for mercy and find mercy freely given do we learn to "render the deeds of mercy." Portia reminds us that

". . . in the course of justice, none of us
Should see salvation. We do pray for mercy,

And that same prayer doth teach us all to render
The deeds of mercy."[19]

Do we need to be reminded that the parable of the Good Samaritan was spoken under the eye of eternal consequences? It was spoken in answer to the question: "What shall I do to inherit eternal life?"[20] This is not an academic question, for it is basically a question of the direction of the soul. Indeed it is not an academic question *for this present time.* For it may well be that Christians learning to show mercy in this age will be the leaven for the saving of our time. We must now live with one another on one earth.

The times cry for people to be able to treat one another with mercy, love, and justice, under the fear of a God who shows mercy, love, and justice to us all. Perhaps not since the days of Rome has there arisen so great a need for a people who are like Christians are supposed to be. The world is in revolution. Men will not be bound by exploiting chains. A new sense of dignity is rising. This could be the Christian's greatest hour—if he obeys the strong command of his Lord to love his neighbor as himself and if he prays: "Thy will be done on earth as it is in heaven—and let it begin with me."

Certainly this is not an academic question *for eternity.* Jesus once said that at the Great Judgment, many would be surprised at the things which Heaven counted important: "I was hungry and you gave me food, I was thirsty and you gave me drink, I was a stranger and you welcomed me, I was naked and you clothed me, I was sick and you visited me, I was in prison and you came to me."[21] Heaven counts

". . . that best portion of a good man's life,
His little, nameless, unremembered, acts
Of kindness and of love."[22]

The Jericho road runs everywhere—even through the ghetto and the pogrom—through the homes of the rich and the hovels of the poor. We rub elbows every day with people who need love and compassion. And Christ's strong command still shows them to us: "Who proved neighbor to the man . . . ?"[23] The picture of the Good Samaritan bending over a nameless man can never die. It will be thrust aside at the peril of losing one of those things which hold the world together. The man by the road is a picture of what we all might be. The man bending over him is a picture of what we all ought to be.

CHAPTER XI

Christ's Three Greatest Commands

"I will turn my face to the wind, and cast my handful of seed on high."[1]

CHRIST gave three strong commands from which His followers cannot escape. They embrace the program of the Church and are the summation of the spirit of a Christian. Those three commands may be stated simply in three words: "Go," "Witness," "Serve." A Christian who does not have these three words in his vocabulary has missed the point of Christianity.

"THE FIELD IS THE WORLD"

"The kingdom of heaven may be compared to a man who sowed good seed in his field . . . and the seed should sprout and grow, he knows not how."[2] And "the field," said Jesus, "is the world."[3] But all is not that simple. There is an "enemy" who sows weeds. Both the weeds and the wheat grow until the harvest. "The harvest is the close of the age."[4] So Jesus in a simple parable embraced the age and the work of His followers in that age: "*Go* therefore and make disciples of all nations . . ."[5]

We are commanded to go and sow good seed: truth, goodness, mercy, faith, hope, love, a church here, a mission there, a school, a television program, a radio message. *But we sow in a rebel world.* Flags are raised against us. There is an "enemy" at work also. There is "wheat" and there are "weeds." Poison seed grows with the good—a church in this block but a place of sin in the next. Here walks an upright man, but in the same office a man who will stop at nothing to gain his ends.

Our first reaction is like that of the servants in the parable. We would pull up the weeds! The *Rubáiyát* expresses it for us:

> ". . . could you and I with Him conspire
> To grasp this sorry Scheme of Things entire,
> Would we not shatter it to bits—and then
> Remould it nearer to the Heart's Desire!"[6]

But we are not God—and have not the wisdom to remold the world. And not only that, but who could hope to be spared? Who is entirely free from weeds? Better to listen to God: "Let both grow together until the harvest . . . lest in gathering the weeds you root up the wheat along with them."[7]

But if we sow in a rebel world, *we sow with courage.* "Until the harvest"—all history bears this sign. The enemy sows his seeds of pride, greed, ambition, selfishness, lust, prejudice. The catalogue is probably without end. The fruits of evil grow up in the world. There are wars, broken homes, blood and tears—the bitter issue of man's inhumanity to man. Evil comes mysteriously—"while men were sleeping." No one has ever solved the problem of evil. Jesus did not attempt to solve it for us. He assumed it, and faced the fact.

The dreadful drama has an end. There is a "harvest." A period is to be placed. A curtain is to be rung down. The theologian calls this the doctrine of "last things." Jesus is saying that we cannot assume time will continue forever. There will be a period. There are, of course, many intermediate "harvests" in history. Waterloo was a harvest. The death of Hitler and the Third Reich was a harvest. But there will be a final harvest. At the end two pictures: the evil gathered out, the sickle thrust in, the weeds cast into a "furnace of fire." We cannot possibly know the full reality of what this means: "The Son of man will send his angels, and they will gather out of his kingdom all causes of sin and all evildoers . . . Then the righteous will shine like the sun in the kingdom of their Father. He who has ears, let him hear."[8]

But in the meantime, shall we abandon our efforts? No, *we sow with hope*. We sow, sleep and rise, and find growth. But the growth is not of our doing. This is our constant humility as well as our hope. George Buttrick has reminded us that the story of the farmer who boasted that you should have seen the field when the Lord had it by Himself is a poor parable and its point fails.[9] For that field was blessed by the Lord with sun, shower, and soil. They were there when the man came and planted his seed; and without those things he would have had no harvest. The surgeon will tell us that there is such a thing as "medical grace." He will use his skill, but then he must depend upon the God-given restoring powers of the body. There is a "grace" in the world—a growing and restoring power not of ourselves. And we must acknowledge again and again that we sow and sleep and the seed springs up and grows we know not how. We know not, that is, until we look up to a beneficent Father.

So the missionary enterprise of the Christian Church, at home and abroad, is conducted in this hope. The Church itself was a little "seed" planted in a hostile world. Everything was against the growth of the Church—everything, that is, except God. So we go and sow with a prayer to Him who gives the increase. We go before the face of the angels who wait to thrust in their sickles for the harvest. Upon the field of the world, the Christian is commanded to sow Christ, who is peace, where there was war; pardon where there was the shadow of condemnation; change where there was stagnation; resurrection where there was doom.

"GOD SO LOVED THE WORLD"

Some years ago a splendid new post office building was built in one of our large cities. Impressive opening ceremonies were held, many dignitaries were present for the occasion. Someone made an important speech. But in the midst of all the festivities, a small boy's voice was heard: "Daddy, where can I mail a letter?" Then to the extreme embarrassment of all concerned, it was discovered that there actually was no place in all that great post office building to mail a letter!

The point is that when we speak of this whole matter of the world mission of the Church, we must not forget the heart of the matter, the place to mail the letter. Where is the heart? In the words of a beloved text written in crimson: "For God so loved the world that he gave his only Son . . ."[10] We meet here with something ultimate in the Christian Faith. Christ commanded us to "Go," but God came first. The mission of men was preceded by the mission of God.

The disciple is brought to an inescapable responsibility. He has the responsibility of the world. He is commanded to "Go." Sometimes he must go himself. Sometimes he can only give money that others might go. It may mean sons and daughters. It always means prayer. And behind all this there must be a conviction—a heart-based belief—that the world through Him can be saved; that the world through Him ought to be saved; that we will do our part.

We propagate what we believe. This is an axiom of life. We propagate what we believe, and what we believe is vital to ourselves and other people. Witness the millions the United States has spent to propagate democracy. The gospel of American capitalism is preached throughout the world at huge cost—because the American people believe in it as a way of life, and because we believe it is vital to our very preservation. In 1812 the Massachusetts legislature was debating a bill to incorporate a new mission board, and a great deal of opposition arose. One of the legislators speaking in opposition is reported to have said: "The country has no religion to spare!" Perhaps he was closer to the truth than he knew.

"YOU SHALL BE MY WITNESSES"

"You shall be my witnesses . . . to the end of the earth."[11] That strong command has not been revoked. We are to "go" and "witness." Obviously one thing that meets us first about the command to witness is that it is the *Lord's command.* It is not a dictum of a church council. The command to witness is recorded as His last command. Every Gospel closes on this note. Matthew has: "Go therefore and make disciples of all nations."[12] Among the closing words of Luke are: "You are witnesses of these things."[13] The Gospels end not with a period but with a dash. They are merely prologues, prefaces to that which the disciples of Christ would do through the Holy Spirit.

Jesus looked at ordinary people and said, "You are the light of the world."[14] Familiarity with this word has taken much of its glory. Yet this magnificent commission to be His witnesses cannot be equaled by the commission of any king or queen on earth. And the apostles had no other explanation for their fantastic behavior than that they were carrying out His command: "We cannot but speak the things which we have seen and heard." . . . "This Jesus hath God raised up, whereof we all are witnesses."[15] So they went out into the streets and proclaimed Him Lord and King of the world.

Thereafter until now, the Gospel of Christ has been spread by the simple expedient which Jesus began—by the word of one person to another. Many have died being witnesses. Indeed the Greek word for witness means "martyr." The blood of the "martyrs" has been the seed of the Church. It was the Lord's strong command, and they could not escape it.

Moreover, witnessing is *the only way to power and effectiveness in the Church.* The Church can have many things and miss the point. There can be beautiful appointments, well-organized committees and study groups, excellent financial campaigns and drives, and still no "place to mail a letter," so to speak. Beautiful appointments are always needed in the Lord's church. There is a place for organization. But the church does not propagate herself by these means. When a church dies, it is not usually for lack of organization or money, or of special campaigns. When a church dies, it is for lack of an evangelistic fervor in her members—for lack of those who remember the strong command of Christ to witness to Him.

The ancient church at Ephesus has been immortalized in the book of Revelation. It must have been a splendid church. It is described as a church of works, toil, patient endurance, and one that could not bear evil men.[16] In other words, it was a working, organized church, zealous for the orthodoxy of the faith. But there was a dreadful omission. They had left their "first love."[17] And what is the first love of any Christian or any church? Not its place in the community—but Jesus Christ!

Marxist Communism has stolen from Christianity its main medium of evangelism—the principle of individual Christian witnessing. From the days of the apostles, the Gospel of Christ has been spread by one Christian to an individual non-Christian. It was spread by little groups of Christians meeting wherever they could and witnessing to friends and neighbors. If we are to beat the Communists, there is at least one thing we must do, and that is return to our original level and tactics. The Christian dare not keep silence any longer in the market place, lest he wake up one day to find that someone has clapped a hand over his mouth. There is no power in a name or a building or a denomination. Great names and great buildings and great denominations have contributed great things. But the power has been in the individual witness of the Christian who has not forgotten his "first love."

How shall we witness? This is a reasonable question. The average Christian is neither a preacher nor a missionary. But he is not exempt. We can witness first, of course, by our *money*. Let us not shrink from the word. The giving of money is the easiest way to witness. It is like paying a soldier to take our place in the wars.

We witness to our faith in Christ and His Kingdom by a *life of faith,* by the way we stand up against life and in life. The non-Christian looks at the Christian: How does he stand up when life hits him? The strength of the steel is tested in battle, not lying on a shelf. How we stand in crisis is often one of the most powerful ways of being a witness to Christ. Many a sermon has been preached in this way without words.

Again, we witness by the *example of love*. "A new commandment I give to you," said Jesus to His disciples, "that you love one another . . ."[18] "By this"—not by the sign in front of your church, nor by proclamation or resolution, but "by this all men will know that you are my disciples."[19] There's nothing worse than a church fight! So the common saying goes outside the church. We should blush at the suggestion. It is too close to the truth. Chips on shoulders apparently are considered by some in the church as part of "the whole armor of God." The first Christians wrung this grudging compliment from their pagan enemies: "Behold, how these Christians love one another!" Not even a Rembrandt can paint a picture of love or mercy. But here is a man or woman of love and mercy, walking abroad. Theirs is a powerful witness.

We witness also by the testimony of a *righteous life*. A righteous life is not prudery or piosity. It is walking "rightly" with God and our fellows. Business, professional, and social practices speak louder than words; and preach sermons seven days a week.

Finally, we witness by *personal testimony*. We cannot avoid the direct word from one person to another. Of course we are not to be bombastic or offensive. No one wishes to be collared and asked, "Brother, are you saved?" That kind of attitude usually drives people away. The witness must be given gently, in the spirit of Christ. And there are times when the Christian must not be silent. His life will often speak, but there are times when his tongue must speak. There are times when the word must be spoken: "Sir, may I introduce you to my Master, Jesus Christ?"

Here a word to the layman: You are there, in the world of business, the professional world, the world of labor, the world of selling. Elton Trueblood has reminded us that there is a gap between work and Christian vocation today.[20] That gap must be bridged by the layman. It is bridged in part by the layman witnessing to Christ in his daily world. The layman is in a position to do this, when the clergyman is not. Here the layman can do far more than the clergyman. The layman's word is an "unprofessional" word, and gains a more ready hearing. This is perhaps one of the most exciting new fields for the Christian layman in the twentieth century. He is virtually on his own. There are no books to guide him, except the New Testament. There is no one to inspire him on Monday morning, except Jesus Christ.

A question might properly be asked here: Who creates a secular society? Is it the pagan? We cannot blame him, for this is his nature. Could it be the Christian who segments his religion? He is devout upon one occasion; but when he enters the door of his business or takes up the tools of his profession or labors at his daily work, his religion is something that is far away. The presence of one Christian can often make the difference between a secular and a Christian situation. The Christian might well consider whether or not it is he who has created this secular vacuum in society, by his own division of his faith from his work.

Once long ago a group of people were standing around a fire in a yard outside a courtroom. Standing near the fire was a bulk of a man, trying to warm himself and, at the same time, pull back into the shadows and hide his face. His big, gnarled fisherman's hands were clasped nervously behind him. A little serving maid tripped across the courtyard and pointed her finger at Simon Peter and said: "I know you. You're one of His disciples!" And Peter drew back and glanced nervously at the soldiers standing nearby. "No, no," he said. "Yes," she said, "you are. You're from Galilee, I can tell by your accent. You're one of the Galileans who follow Jesus of Nazareth who is on trial now for His life." And Peter said loudly, "No, I'm not!" Again, with an oath, "No!"[21] So, as Halford Luccock has reminded us, Peter denied the best thing that had ever happened in his life.[22]

The world will know the Christian by his "accent," by the accent of his speech and by the accent of his life. "Are not you also one of this man's disciples?"[23] The question will be put; and our lives, our money, our word will answer. We shall deny Him, or we shall obey His strong command.

THE LOST WORD

We have lost a word today. Indeed, it is more an idea than a word, for to put it in a word limits its boundaries. The word is "service." The strong command of Christ was to "go," "witness," and "serve." Service is a poor word to describe this great Christian idea. Service is giving oneself to others; going the second mile, giving good measure pressed down and running over; loving our enemies; giving without wondering what we shall get in return; being merciful to others, being slow to judge.

Our time has made the word menial. Service is something beneath us. It means being a servant, which is the next thing to being a slave. "Which is greater," said Jesus, "one who sits at table, or one who serves?"[24] The answer was obvious then as now: "Is it not the one who sits at table?"[25] Obviously, he who is served is greater. This is the standard of the world.

Dr. Albert Einstein, in his last recorded interview, had this to say about our time: "He is considered successful in our time who gets more out of life than he puts in." In this Dr. Einstein has uncomfortably evaluated our time. Too often the current standard of success is, "What are you getting?" And the current formula for living is, "How little can I get by on for how much?" The words we are using show how we are thinking: "benefits," "security," "compensation." Now of course there is nothing wrong with just benefits, reasonable security, and rightful compensation. But the seeking of these things can obscure the strong command of Christ to serve. The work is on a cost plus basis, so work as slowly as possible. The expense account can be padded and no one will be the wiser. Advertise the product with half-truths, for what matter, just so the product is sold? Let the hammer slip, and let the goods be shoddy. He that sits at table is greater than he that serves. Therefore, let us seek to be served.

In a sentence and by His own example, Jesus sweeps this philosophy away: "But I am among you as one who serves."[26] The Christian must not only listen to his Lord; he must also look at Him. He wears no crown, but is girded with a towel and kneels in the place of a slave. "You call me Teacher and Lord; and you are right, for so I am. If I then, your Lord and Teacher, have washed your feet, you also ought to wash one another's feet. For I have given you an example . . ."[27] Then gently He reminds us of this proud and sophisticated twentieth century: "A servant is not greater than his master."[28] The Christian cannot take a higher place than his Lord. He cannot sit at meat while his Lord serves. When he looks for his place, he finds it beside the Lord of the towel and basin. "He who is greatest among you shall be your servant."[29]

A national news magazine carried a delightful story of the little girl who had an interview with the Pope in Rome. He asked her what she had seen. She replied in all innocence that she had been looking for God; but that all she had seen were many churches, stained-glass windows, and pillars! So we can look for God and miss Him in stained-glass windows, pillars, and magnificent architecture. These are simply evidences of man's gratitude to God. We must search until we find One whose countenance is lowly, whose hands are gnarled in service, who is kneeling somewhere at some menial task of love. For there we have found God. "Even as the Son of man came not to be served, but to serve, and to give his life as a ransom for many."[30]

The world's truly great have been servants. They had no banners borne before them and no plaques dedicated to their memory: a man and woman who give themselves to each other all their days and thus make a bright spot upon earth's spotted surface; a home made bright by father's toil and mother's love; a man who forsook wealth and labored at a humbler task that he might not lose himself, but give himself to those around him; a faithful teacher; the man or woman who walked in compassion and who touched the lives of others with a benediction. These are the unsung greats. Jesus said that those who give themselves in service shall be the greatest. And perhaps even before the Great Throne, they will in modesty prefer that their names not be called.

This service is the way to real *happiness*. Real happiness does not lie in the comfortable avoidance of life, but in meeting life full and giving the best to it, whether to family, profession, church, or nation. Life must be met, not avoided with a tranquilizing pill. Soon the pill will wear off and life will still be waiting.

No one has ever come forward to answer the question of Jesus: "For what can a man give in return for his life?"[31] What will a man give in exchange for that part of him that lives forever? That part of him that can be set downward upon the path of greed, lust, and selfishness—or upward upon the path of service, giving, love, and compassion? Jesus once looked at a man who had it all—houses, lands, and barns—and over his life wrote this terrible epitaph: "Thou fool . . ."[32]

One of the great scenes of literature is the interview between Marley and Scrooge in Dickens' *Christmas Carol.* Jacob Marley, Scrooge's partner in life, has come up out of hell, dragging his account books, safes, and moneybags in an endless chain. He calls upon Scrooge to repent. Scrooge, hearing that terrible voice out of hell, falters: "But you were always a good man of business, Jacob." "Business!" replied Marley, wringing his hands. "Mankind was my business."[33] To forget that, regardless of our business or profession, is a dreadful omission. It is to let something slip away a little at a time. It is to forget day after day the acts of kindness and of mercy, until one day we awaken to discover that something precious has slipped away from us, like a summer's day in our youth which cannot be recalled.

"Go ye into all the world . . . You shall be my witnesses . . . He who is greatest among you shall be your servant."[34] The Christian will always find it difficult to forget the strong example of Him who took a cross and served the world. He will find it difficult to forget these strong commands. He will forget at very peril of his soul.

CHAPTER XII

Under the Eye of Eternity

"That God, which ever lives and loves,
One God, one law, one element,
And one far-off divine event,
To which the whole creation moves."

TENNYSON[1]

PERHAPS one day Jesus and His disciples were walking down a street in Jerusalem and came upon a caravan drawn up before one of the great houses of the city. Out of the house comes the master himself, followed by two or three stewards to whom he is giving last-minute instructions. Farther down the street, they may have come upon another caravan returning from one of the cities of the East. The lord of that house alights from his camel and the stewards of the house rush out to greet him. Some have great joy on their faces. Some are reluctantly hanging back. Others are running up late, arranging their clothing in a decent appearance, flushed and hot of face because they are not ready.

Jesus turns to His disciples and waves His hand toward that common picture of the time and says: "The kingdom of heaven . . . will be as when a man going on a journey called his servants and entrusted to them his property . . ."[2] The parable of the talents is a familiar one. It is a story which Jesus plucked from life to illustrate a piercing truth: The parable reminds us first that *we inhabit the earth and time in humble tenantry*. We are servants left with the substance of the world. God has entrusted to us His "goods"—the earth with its treasure store, time's precious minutes and hours, strength of arm and brain, courage of soul and heart; and those invaluable coins of mercy, love, and faith.

TO ONE FIVE, TO ANOTHER TWO

Our talents are manifestly not the same: to one five, to another two, to another one. There is a Shakespeare's brain and there is a man with printer's art to bring the product of that brain to the world. There is a speaker's tongue and a man to pull switches and string wires that his message may be carried on the air. There is a musician's voice and the man who prints upon the page the notes which he himself cannot sing. There is the man with the capacity to plan, and a man who labors in his factory. There is a mother with the gift of love, and a son who walks strong upon the earth and does great deeds. There is a Rembrandt, and a carpenter to make the frame. There is a Paul to preach and a Luke to minister in the background. There is a Livingstone to pioneer, with a faithful black man to follow him and finally to carry him back in simple dignity to Westminster Abbey. Whatever we are—of brain, strength, substance, or talent—we have upon loan by the Lord of heaven and earth. We inhabit earth and time in humble tenantry.

A TIME OF RECKONING

So then there must be *a time of reckoning*. The lord of the house sits down and his stewards range themselves before him: "Now after a long time the master of those servants came and settled accounts with them."[3] Books were opened, accounts made; and the dreaded or joyously awaited questions were asked.

The poor wretch who buried his talent in the ground was, he said, afraid. "What can one man do?" he said. So he was afraid to trust, to venture. Such a man thinks mercy and charity are signs of weakness. He fears to sow in the fields of the world and trust God to give the increase. He is afraid to bear witness to the God-given convictions within him lest he be trampled by the mob. He buries the part he should have had in prayer, in worship, in devotion, in giving.

The man who buries his talent would be content with the routine of his church; afraid to have his church stand on new frontiers of evangelism or range itself alongside the banners of truth, justice, and righteousness. He would bury his Christ in a hymn on Sunday, lest he take Him to the office with him on Monday. He would hang the cross about his neck as an article of jewelry but fear to bear that cross before him like the courageous banner it has always been. He would hoard comfortably the precious truths of Christianity, as he likes to call them, and be fearful of letting them get into his living room or sit down with him at his desk.

There must be a time of reckoning, and *God expects an increase*. What was done with the "talent" given us? The Biblical talent has been reckoned at approximately a thousand dollars. For us, it may be talent of coin or brain or time. It may be the hour that will not return; the ability to reach a merciful hand; or the ability to pray.

So then we must face a question: What was done with the coin that was only a token—something of earth loaned to us for a time? The blessing of church and sacrament is a talent of Heaven loaned for a season. And we are stewards of earth and sea and sky. The "lord of the house" will demand a reckoning. The things that are the most important to us are the things to which we give our time, talents, and money. Are they important to the Lord of the House?

The oldest living thing discovered on earth is a four-thousand-year-old bristle-cone pine, found in the White Mountains of California.[4] For four millenniums that pine has been there on the summit of those lofty mountains; while history was made, while nations rose and fell, while Jesus Christ was crucified, while the apostles set out on their missionary journeys. All the time that old tree was clinging stubbornly to the side of the mountain, sinking its roots, drawing out substance and nurture from mother earth! Far better to have been an old oak tree where boys climbed in an abandon of joy. Its shade was always there when the day was hot. And someone grieved when the storm cut it down. Far better to have been that old oak tree that lived, comparatively speaking, only a short span, than that bristle-cone pine, still gnarled and clinging to the earth—and producing not one thing in blessing.

The story of Jesus cursing a fig tree takes us aback. The fig tree is barren and gives no promise whatsoever of producing fruit in return for the nurture and substance of God's green earth. The tree is cursed. It is a parable of life, a stern lesson: That which does not give back something of what has been given to it is cursed with impotence, with joylessness, with the dark frown of the God who created not a getting universe, but a creating and a giving universe. "What talent is born in you?" asks Carlyle. "How do you employ that?" This matter is so big and all-embracing that we can only compare it to the over-arching Kingdom of God that embraces all things.

Now God is not a harsh and implacable landlord like the earthly landowners in Jesus' time. The parable must not be pushed too far. Jesus would never liken God to those earthly landlords, with their meannesses. For He prayed to a gentle Father in heaven. Yet a sharp fact emerges here: God does expect a reckoning and an accounting of our faithfulness with what we have been given. He will be unrestrained in His commendation of faithfulness: "Well done, good and faithful servant . . ." He will be gentle with the man who did the best he could with what he had. The two-talent man received exactly the same commendation as the five-talent man. Surely, if the one-talent man had been faithful with that which had been committed to him, he would have received the same commendation as the other two.

The frown of God is upon the man who selfishly hoards himself or what he has, who fears to venture for God, who complains that he has not been given enough. He hoards his store of love and never ranges himself alongside the standards of truth and justice. He keeps his coin (whether coin minted by the government or coin minted by God) clutched in miser's grasp until it and he perish.

And what shall be said of the man who forgets, who does not even bother to remember that he has a Lord? Even the one-talent man in the parable recognized all along that his lord was the rightful owner of the talent. Or did he forget, too? Did he forget when a long time went by and his lord tarried? Did he forget and lull himself into a false sense of security that he could do what he pleased with what he had?

If the parable stabs us awake to a sharper examination of our stewardship, it should. It reminds us, clearly and forcibly, that we live and we work and we give under the eye of eternity. Part of the strong command of God is to remember our stewardship under Him. It is God who will be sitting on the throne and saying, "As you did it to one of the least of these my brethren, you did it to me."[5] It is He who will come forward and draw us into the joy of heaven. And we shall want no other palm or crown save the accolade of the King: "Well done, good and faithful servant; you have been faithful over a little, I will set you over much."[6] And when we hesitate on that joyous threshold and think surely we must ask forgiveness for so many things, He will come forward and draw us across and say, "Enter into the joy of your master."[7]

"WHY THIS WASTE?"

But to give is a waste to some. They still subscribe to the creed that a man is here to get all he can and keep all he can, whether it be coin of substance or coin of heart. Worship is a waste of time and prayer is an idleness. The Bible is a book of stories for children to learn. Let fools throw their lives away upon some distant mission field. Let the preacher preach. An honest man must make a living! He cannot afford the luxury of love and compassion. And justice is only a word—a statue that is blind.

There is a little story that needs to be retold. While the shadows were closing around Jesus and evil counsel was being taken to destroy Him, a little drama was enacted. It is a story that is sometimes forgotten in all the great bustling events of the Passion Week. But it will be told again and again. It is the story of the alabaster jar.[8]

Jesus was at a dinner party in Bethany. His host was Simon the Leper, possibly one whom Jesus had cured of that terrible disease and who still retained the name out of habit. During the course of the meal, "a woman," says the record, "came up to him."[9] She will always remain one of the world's unknowns. Her deed is crystal-clear, but her face remains in the shadows. Perhaps she was Mary Magdalene, from whom Jesus cast seven devils. Perhaps she was one whom Jesus had redeemed to a life of decency and honor. Her name does not matter. Her deed is that which lives.

She bore a costly gift. The alabaster jar of perfume has been valued at approximately three hundred denarii, which in those days would have been the equivalent of an entire year's wages. There was silence as she approached Jesus. Some frowned and bit their lips in vexation at this unwarranted intrusion. They hoped she would present her gift and leave as quickly as possible in order that the embarrassment in the atmosphere might be cleared. And then the people in that room saw something that they would not believe. For the woman was kneeling and opening the jar and was actually pouring the contents over the head of Jesus! And for a moment, the whole group froze in a kind of silent tableau.

Now everyone in that room missed the point of that scene—even the disciples. The immediate reaction was righteous indignation. A murmur of strong disapproval went up around the room. "What a waste!" they said. "For this ointment might have been sold for a large sum, and given to the poor." The equivalent of a whole year's wage poured upon the head of a man! And so they gestured self-righteously toward the poor; and probably the poor actually were clustered about the doors of Simon's house. It was the custom to allow the poor in the city to come upon such an occasion and afterwards to receive any of the crumbs that might be left from the rich man's table.

So the poor were probably there, their pinched faces peering in the windows. The guests gestured self-righteously toward the poor, but there is no indication that any of them made a move toward his pocketbook to give even one denarius for the poor. They merely murmured, "Why this waste?"[10] And they thought they had practicality on their side. A righteous murmur and sternly disapproving looks were directed toward the woman and Jesus.

Would Jesus rebuke her too? We must learn something from the fact that He did not. "Why do you trouble the woman? For she has done a beautiful thing to me."[11] Underscore the phrase "a beautiful thing." Is not one point of this little story the fact that God makes place in His world for the sheer waste of beauty?[12] Why not leave off the flowers and make all the land produce grain? Why not smooth down the mountaintops into one monotonous plain and leave off the towering peaks and the strong silent places of the earth? Why not drain the seas and leave off the thundering roar of the surf? Why has God flung into the universe myriads of stars that apparently have no utilitarian value whatsoever? But God has set sheer beauty in the world like a jewel.

Love is a waste to some, but without it we would live like animals. Faith is a waste to many, but without it we would walk blindly and without hope on this earth. Gratitude is a waste to some, but without it we would all be churls. One of the joys of life is the ability to appreciate beauty, else why do we long for another spring? Why put a church in the midst of a city? Why not put up a skyscraper dedicated to commerce and trade? Indeed why put a church anywhere? The breaking of the alabaster jar was like all of these things

—sheer beauty. True, it fed not a single mouth; but it was like God placing a flower where others might have put grain. "She has done a beautiful thing."

Now, of course, this is not to say that we shall blithely turn our backs upon the poor in contemplation of beauty. This story gives no excuse for that; for Jesus, by example and by saying, showed us the poor. He said that in the Last Judgment mention would be made of the cup of cold water, of the sick visited, of the naked clothed and the hungry fed. But are not these, too, "beautiful things"?

True devotion is never a waste, whether to God or man. It is not waste to give to Christ if that gift springs from devotion. Time spent in service or worship or prayer is never wasted. Money given that His church might be beautifully appointed is never wasted. The great cathedrals, chapels, and churches are the breaking of someone's alabaster jar of love and devotion for Jesus Christ. It is true that Notre Dame Cathedral has never produced a single machine or gadget of any kind; but what it represents in devotion to Christ can only be measured by eternity. Your church and mine is not bricks and stone, but broken alabaster jars. What would be left if, in a fit of anger or folly, we decided to strip the world of all the beauty that has been given and done in the name of Christ? The missionary's devotion is sometimes looked upon with pitying or condescending eye, but God sees it as the breaking of an alabaster jar. The martyr's blood was sheer waste to the Roman cynic, but later thought called it "the seed of the Church."

Such beauty is never really lost. "Truly, I say to you, wherever this gospel is preached in the whole world, what she has done will be told in memory of her."[13] Her deed was not lost, not pathetically thrown away in a beautiful though useless gesture. She was not anointing a lost cause. Her story is "told" again and again; and her deed is a perpetual memorial.

The great example is staring us in the face—the sheer

"waste" of the cross of Jesus Christ. It was a waste to many —the waste of a good life with all its potentialities. But God took the cross and made it more than a living memorial. It was made a living power. For upon the cross, Christ broke the alabaster jar of His life. And though we say the words, they are too poor to describe the gift: "For God so loved the world that he gave his only Son."[14]

There is a parenthesis to the story, a kind of tragic post-script. Immediately after this incident, records Matthew, there is another item of money mentioned: not only three hundred denarii, but thirty pieces of silver! We hardly need ask the question: "Which was lost, the alabaster jar of devotion or the thirty pieces of betrayal?" Judas' story is told, too; but in a kind of horrible memorial of the base Judean who, it could be said, "threw a pearl away richer than all his tribe."[15]

"Why this waste?" But which is more wasteful—to take the substance of God and clutch it selfishly or fling it away upon the earth, or to use it as a sacred trust from the Lord of all life? The woman and her alabaster jar shame us. The little earthen jar continues to shine with an unyielding light in the darkness of the years, a reminder that the beauty of love and faith, the beauty of sheer devotion given, are most precious in the eyes of God. The greatest waste of eternity is a starved and shriveled soul.

"HE WHO SOWS BOUNTIFULLY"

There is no law that compels how much we shall give of ourselves or our money, but there is another law: "He who sows sparingly will also reap sparingly, and he who sows bountifully will also reap bountifully."[16] This is not an appeal to self-interest. The New Testament has never said, "Tithe and you will be successful and prosperous." There is a blessing in tithing; but not everyone who tithes is guaranteed to become a millionaire, or finds his business automatically growing.

But this is still one of nature's basic laws: "He who sows sparingly will also reap sparingly." He who sows a grudging seed will reap a grudging harvest. Jesus said: "The measure you give will be the measure you get."[17] Give a grudging measure of love to the world, and we will get a grudging measure of love. Sow revenge, hatred, bitterness, and we will reap a similar harvest. Sow goodness, charity, and mercy and the harvest will be joyous. Give a grudging measure of ourselves, our money, and our time to the Church and then let us not be surprised if the blessings of the fellowship and worship of the Church pass us by. The universe is "moral" and a just God is in control. The scales have a way of balancing.

UNDER THE OPEN HAND OF GOD

We give under the open hand of God. "God is able," said Paul, "to provide you with every blessing in abundance, so that you may always have enough of everything and may provide in abundance for every good work."[18] God is able. The Christian does not give in fear for his own security. The story of the widow who fed Elijah and found her food supply constantly replenished is more than a miracle confined to a few measures of oil.[19] It is God's way of saying that there is written into the very fabric of the universe a law of divine generosity. The hand of God is always open, and the Christian gives with an open hand, knowing that the open hand of God is always above him: "If you then, who are evil, know how to give good gifts to your children, how much more will your Father who is in heaven . . . ?"[20] "Consider the lilies . . . Look at the birds of the air . . . your heavenly Father feeds them. Are you not of more value than they?"[21] We are still like children going about this universe and discovering the glory and the blessing of a prodigal God who has spread with a prodigal hand blessings that will be for us and for generations to come.

"God is able to provide you with every blessing in abundance, so that you may always have enough of everything and may provide in abundance for every good work."[22] God blesses in order that we may bless. He expects the same largeness and generosity from His children. The Certain Rich Man is called fool; not because he had possessions, but because in all those full and overflowing barns there was not room enough for a corresponding largeness of soul.[23]

We live under the eye of eternity, and it is a blessed eye. We give under the eye of eternity. But God never bargains. His sunlight will skip across the fields of the just and unjust man. Neither does He promise crowns and jewels in return for our offerings of either mercy or coin. The humbling truth is that in proportion to His gifts ours make a poor show. Our few coins and hours given are paltry indeed. Even the largeness of our hearts toward others is small beside the large heart of God. Yet it is possible that He cherishes what we give to Him of coin and time and prayer far, far more than He cherishes the praise of all the angels and archangels in highest heaven.

A Word After

"YOU have not passed this way before."[1] This very second is a new path. The thought was frightening to Israel when Joshua first spoke these words. The Jordan lay before them. More than that, it was rumored that there were giants across the Jordan. Jericho was there, too; and that walled city looked impregnable. Then, if that were not enough, the Hittites, the Hivites, the Amorites, the Perizzites, and all the rest were waiting!

The giants of the future are the biggest giants of all. We face national giants—cold war, atomic fallout, inflation, and guided missiles. Race relations plague the national scene. We have our personal giants to face. Some kind of Jordan rolls before every person who reads this page. Some giant waits for battle.

The Jordan has to be crossed. The great trumpet of ram's horn sounded the assembly, and the children of Israel knew they had to move forward. *And the Ark went in front.* What was the Ark? Probably it was a boxlike affair with two angels carved overhead. Tradition has it that inside the Ark were a copy of the Ten Commandments, some manna from wilderness days, and the rod of Moses. *It was their shrine*—in other words, the focal point of their faith in God's law and mercy.

It is significant that Joshua commanded the Ark to be carried in front of the people as they crossed the Jordan.

So they followed their shrine and believed that God went before them. *They believed God was in tomorrow.* "For," said Joshua, "tomorrow the Lord will do wonders among you."[2] We cannot cross the Jordan unless our shrine goes with us. Jordan will roll up black and impenetrable sometimes, and we will be afraid to put our feet in the water. This is the time to keep our shrine in sight—to remember that God goes before us, and God is able. This is the time to pray the ancient prayer of Moses, when the Ark was lifted to the shoulders of the priests and Israel began to march: "Rise up, Lord, and let thine enemies be scattered."[3]

Here is a parenthesis. A study of Israel's history reveals that after they crossed the Jordan, they put down their Ark in Shiloh and went off and left it there. The rest of the story is one trouble after another. A long time after, David remembered the Ark and went back to Shiloh and brought it to Jerusalem. There is a parable here. Many a person has gone off and left his Ark—left the focal point of his faith and gone about the affairs of the world. Distress has come and there has been nothing to bring courage and faith. And no wonder—*he left his shrine behind him.*

But only Jordan must be crossed in a day. Never mind about Jericho and the Hittites. Your job today is to cross the Jordan. *God calls us to the day before us and the task at hand.* The battle of Jericho must wait for another day. The giants of tomorrow must wait their turn. Emerson in one of his more penetrating moments wrote: "It is one of the illusions that the present hour is not the critical decisive hour; write it on your hearts that every day is the best day of the year. No man has learned anything rightly until he knows that every day is doom's day."

The most difficult thing to do is to do the common thing that lies at hand. The difficult thing is to decide today that I shall cast my life for the right, and let the giant of tomorrow come when he will. The simple and ordinary task of today must be done honestly and sincerely. If this is done, tomorrow's giants are not nearly so large. We must live faithfully today, and let the problem of tomorrow assume the proportions that it will. The strength derived from living today will be the strength added for living tomorrow. Jesus taught us to pray for our bread today.

It would be flowery to say that the centuries stand before us, but they do not. Not even the years stand before us. Not even tomorrow stands before us, but only today. And the day is in God's hands. The hands of God are now pierced for our transgressions. He has dwelt among us and His eyes have looked upon this common earthly scene. We have not passed this way before. But God has. He is still our shield and guiding star—a pillar of fire by night and a cloud by day. By this strong comfort we are led beyond Jordan to a Promised Land.

Notes and Acknowledgments

A WORD BEFORE

1. G. K. Chesterton, "The Romance of Orthodoxy," from *The Everlasting Man*. Reprinted by permission of Dodd, Mead & Company from *The Man Who Was Chesterton*, p. 403. Edited by Raymond T. Bond. Copyright © 1932 by Dodd, Mead & Company, Inc.
2. See George Buttrick's *Christ and Man's Dilemma*, pp. 30-31. Nashville: Abingdon-Cokesbury Press, 1946.
3. T. S. Eliot, *The Rock*, Part I. New York: Harcourt, Brace and Company, 1934. Used by permission.
4. Karl Barth, *The Word of God and the Word of Man*, p. 190. Tr. by Douglas Horton. Harper Torchbook edition, 1957. By permission of the author and Harper & Brothers, publishers.

PART ONE

Chapter I

DIVINE PITY AND HUMAN FEAR

1. Walter Rauschenbusch, "The Postern Gate," from D. R. Sharpe, *Walter Rauschenbusch*, pp. 451-452. Copyright, 1942, by The Macmillan Company. Reprinted by permission of the author.
2. Psalm 27:1. Unless otherwise indicated the Scripture quotations are from the Revised Standard Version. Copyright 1946, 1952, by Division of Christian Education of the National Council of the Churches of Christ in the U. S. A.
3. Psalm 27:1.
4. Psalm 103:13.
5. Fëdor Dostoevski.
6. Psalm 103:17.
7. Job 15:11.
8. Euripides, *The Trojan Women*.

9. Deuteronomy 33:27.
10. Psalm 18:6.
11. Jude 24.
12. Alfred Tennyson, *Harold,* Act III, Scene ii, lines 114-115.
13. From "Abide With Me," by Henry F. Lyte (1820).
14. John 14:8.
15. Exodus 33:18.
16. Exodus 33:20.
17. Exodus 33:23.
18. Exodus 33:19.
19. Psalm 103:14.
20. Hymn, "He Hideth My Soul."
21. John 1:18.
22. 2 Corinthians 4:6.
23. Matthew 6:32.
24. From the Nicene Creed.
25. Matthew 6:25.
26. Matthew 6:30.
27. Matthew 6:32.
28. Luke 11:9.
29. Luke 11:13; Matthew 7:11.
30. Matthew 10:31; 12:12.
31. Matthew 10:28.
32. John Bunyan, *Pilgrim's Progress,* Part II, Conclusion.
33. Christina Rossetti, "When My Heart Is Vexed I Will Complain," from Songs for Strangers and Pilgrims in *The Poetical Works of Christina Georgina Rossetti.* London: Macmillan and Co., Ltd., 1904, 1924.
34. Luke 19:41.

Chapter II

GOD IS WITH US

1. Isaiah 64:1; Athanasius (293-373), *De Incarnatione Verbe Dei,* Robertson's translation (1884), xliii. From *A Diary of Readings* by John Baillie. New York: Charles Scribner's Sons, 1955. By permission.
2. See Isaiah 7. For a fuller discussion of Isaiah 7:14 see E. L. Stoffel, *His Kingdom Is Forever,* p. 53 ff., Richmond, Va.: John Knox Press, 1956.
3. Isaiah 9:2-6.
4. Isaiah 9:6.
5. Genesis 3:8.
6. Matthew 1:23.
7. Betty W. Stoffel, "His Way," in *Moments of Eternity.* John Knox Press, 1954. By permission.
8. 2 Corinthians 8:9.
9. Matthew 11:28.
10. 2 Corinthians 8:9.
11. John 13:3.
12. John 1:14.
13. Thomas Hardy.
14. G. K. Chesterton, "The House of Christmas." Reprinted by permission of Dodd, Mead & Company from *The Man Who Was Chesterton.* Edited by Raymond T. Bond. Copyright © 1932 by Dodd, Mead & Company, Inc.
15. Matthew 9:36. (K.J.V.)

16. See Matthew 9:32-34.
17. John 2:25. (K.J.V.)
18. Raymond Kresensky, "Christ on Madison Street," No. 335 in *A Treasury of Sermon Illustrations,* edited by Charles L. Wallis. Abingdon Press, 1950. Used by permission.
19. John 10:10. (K.J.V.)
20. See Matthew 6:25.
21. John 1:11.
22. Romans 5:8,6.
23. 1 Peter 1:20.
24. 1 Peter 1:18-20.
25. Robert Browning, *Saul.*

CHAPTER III

GOD'S GREATEST ASSURANCE

1. Saint Augustine.
2. Psalm 51:2-4. (Italics ours.)
3. Isaiah 6:5. (Italics ours.)
4. Isaiah 6:3.
5. Isaiah 6:7.
6. Psalm 51:17.
7. Hosea 11:9. (Italics ours.)
8. Hosea 2:19.
9. Hosea 11:1,3,7,8.
10. Hosea 11:9.
11. Hosea 11:8.
12. Luke 15.
13. Luke 15:12. (K.J.V.)
14. Luke 15:13.
15. Luke 15:18-19.
16. Luke 15:20. (K.J.V.)
17. Hosea 11:8.
18. Luke 15.
19. See Luke 15:4.
20. See Luke 15:8.
21. Luke 15:20.
22. 1 Corinthians 13:4.
23. John 1; 2 Corinthians 8:9.
24. From "The Ninety and Nine," by Elizabeth C. Clephane (1830-1869).
25. George Bernard Shaw.
26. See Luke 18:13.
27. From "The Hound of Heaven," by Francis Thompson (1859-1907).
28. Luke 15:20. (K.J.V.)

CHAPTER IV

THE CONTINUING CHRIST

1. Robert Browning, "Epilogue" (from *Dramatis Personae*).
2. Mark 15:46.
3. Robert Browning, *A Death in the Desert.*
4. Francis Thompson, "The Hound of Heaven."

5. Arthur Hugh Clough, "With Whom Is No Variableness, Neither Shadow of Turning." (1862.)
6. See John 20:26. (K.J.V.)
7. See Revelation 1:18.
8. Luke 24:13-27.
9. Luke 24:21.
10. Luke 24:15.
11. William Cowper, 1779.
12. Acts 1:9.
13. 1 Peter 3:21-22.
14. Ephesians 1:20-21.
15. John 16:7.
16. John 16:8.
17. Hebrews 4:14.
18. Hebrews 4:15.
19. John 14:2.
20. John 14:3.
21. Revelation 1:1.
22. Adam Burnet, *The Lord Reigneth,* p. 127. New York: Charles Scribner's Sons, 1947. London: Hodder & Stoughton, Ltd. Used by permission.
23. Revelation 21:1. (See also *The Revelation of Jesus Christ* by Donald W. Richardson. John Knox Press, 1939.)
24. Revelation 21:4.
25. Source unknown.
26. Revelation 22:3.
27. Matthew Arnold, "A Summer Night."
28. Revelation 21:22.
29. Revelation 21:22; 22:5.
30. Revelation 22:5.
31. John 14:2. (K.J.V.)
32. Revelation 22:3.
33. Rudyard Kipling.
34. Revelation 21:3.
35. 1 Corinthians 13.
36. 2 Corinthians 5:8. (K.J.V.)
37. 1 John 3:2. (K.J.V.)
38. 1 Corinthians 2:9. (K.J.V.)
39. Hebrews 4:16.

PART TWO

Chapter V

THE DISCIPLINE OF FAITH

1. By permission. From Webster's *New Collegiate Dictionary,* copyright 1949, 1951, 1953, 1956 by G. & C. Merriam Company.
2. Isaiah 40:31.
3. Isaiah 40:31.
4. Lord Rosebery, *Miscellanies, Literary and Historical.* London: Hodder & Stoughton, Ltd., 1921. Used by permission.
5. Isaiah 37:38.
6. Lord Byron, "The Destruction of Sennacherib."

7. Isaiah 37:3.
8. Isaiah 36:5.
9. Isaiah 37:4.
10. Isaiah 37:6.
11. 2 Timothy 1:12.
12. As quoted in *Sermons on the Psalms* by Harold A. Bosley, p. 128. New York: Harper & Brothers, 1956. (Originally from a series of articles by Edward R. Murrow, "This I Believe.")
13. Isaiah 37:36.
14. Matthew 17:20.
15. Matthew 17:20.
16. 1 John 3:2.
17. Robert Browning.
18. See *Marching Off the Map,* by Halford E. Luccock, p. 12. Harper & Brothers, 1952. By permission.
19. Mark 9:24. (K.J.V.)
20. George Santayana, "Sonnets, 1883-1893-III," in *Poems.* New York: Charles Scribner's Sons, 1923. By permission.

CHAPTER VI

THE GREAT ANTAGONIST

1. Karl Barth, *Credo,* p. 17. London: Hodder & Stoughton, Ltd., 1936. By permission.
2. Isaiah 6:5.
3. Isaiah 6:7.
4. Isaiah 6:8.
5. Genesis 32.
6. Genesis 32:24. (K.J.V.)
7. Genesis 32:24. (K.J.V.)
8. Genesis 32:26.
9. From "Come, O Thou Traveller, Unknown," by Charles Wesley (1707-1788).
10. Genesis 32:27.
11. Genesis 32:27.
12. Genesis 32:28.
13. Genesis 32:31. (K.J.V.)
14. Genesis 32:30.
15. From "Make Me a Captive, Lord," by George Matheson (1842-1906).
16. Luke 19:5.
17. Luke 19:7.
18. Luke 19:8.
19. Luke 19:9.
20. Luke 19:10.
21. See Revelation 3:21.
22. Lloyd C. Douglas, "The Mirror," in The American Pulpit Series, Book II, p. 74. New York: Abingdon-Cokesbury Press, 1945.

CHAPTER VII

THE GREAT DECISION

1. G. K. Chesterton, "The Romance of Orthodoxy," from *The Everlasting Man.* Reprinted by permission of Dodd, Mead & Company from *The Man*

Who Was Chesterton, p. 399. Edited by Raymond T. Bond. Copyright © 1932 by Dodd, Mead & Company, Inc.
2. 2 Kings 5.
3. 2 Kings 5:12.
4. See Judges 6:36-40.
5. Matthew 16:24.
6. Matthew 16:22.
7. Matthew 16:24.
8. William Shakespeare, *Hamlet,* Act III, Scene 1.
9. Mark 15:34.
10. 1 Corinthians 13:4-7.
11. Luke 23:34.
12. Acts 5:29.
13. Charlotte Stetson Gilman, "A Man Must Live." From *Masterpieces of Religious Verse.* Harper & Brothers, 1948. By permission.
14. From "Love Divine," by Charles Wesley, 1747. (Slightly adapted.)
15. Matthew 16:25-26.
16. Matthew 16:26.
17. Matthew 16:25.
18. Robert Louis Stevenson.
19. Arthur John Gossip, *From the Edge of the Crowd,* p. 168. (Slightly adapted.) Edinburgh: T. & T. Clark, 1924. Used by permission.

Chapter VIII

THE TRIUNE DISCIPLINE

1. Dora Greenwell (1821-1882). From *A Diary of Readings* by John Baillie. New York: Charles Scribner's Sons, 1955. By permission.
2. See Exodus 20:15-16; Matthew 22:37,39; Matthew 5:8-9,7. (K.J.V.)
3. Matthew 17:20. (K.J.V.)
4. 1 John 1:9 (K.J.V.); John 3:17 (R.S.V.).
5. Romans 8:31. (K.J.V.)
6. 1 Samuel 3.
7. Romans 12:20; Luke 10:27.
8. Matthew 5:9.
9. Matthew 5:8.
10. Luke 6:38.
11. Matthew 7:3.
12. Sara Henderson Hay, in "Sic Transit," from *Field of Honor.* The Kaleidograph Press, 1933. Reprinted by permission of author and publishers.
13. John 10:14; John 11:25; Matthew 16:24; John 14:27.
14. Psalm 95:6. (K.J.V.)
15. See Isaiah 6:1.
16. Psalm 51:10.
17. Isaiah 6:5.
18. Isaiah 6:8.
19. 1 Corinthians 1:21. (K.J.V.)
20. See Henry Sloane Coffin's *Communion Through Preaching.* New York: Charles Scribner's Sons, 1952.
21. See Arthur John Gossip's *In the Secret Place of the Most High,* p. 122. New York: Charles Scribner's Sons, 1947. Edinburgh: T. & T. Clark, Ltd. Used by permission.
22. 1 Samuel 3:1. (K.J.V.) (See also R.S.V. rendering.)

23. Isaiah 30:10.
24. John Bunyan, *Pilgrim's Progress,* Part I, "The Celestial City."
25. Luke 18:1.
26. Psalm 51:4.
27. Isaiah 6:8.
28. Matthew 6:32.
29. From the hymn attributed to Reverend George Croly (1780-1860), "Spirit of God, Descend Upon My Heart."

PART THREE

CHAPTER IX

A TIME OUT OF JOINT

1. William Shakespeare, *Hamlet,* Act I, Scene 5, line 189.
2. Jeremiah 20:14. (K.J.V.)
3. Jeremiah 20:18.
4. Jeremiah 20:9.
5. Jeremiah 20:9.
6. Gerard Manley Hopkins, "The Times Are Nightfall," in *Poems of Gerard Manley Hopkins,* edited by Robert Bridges. (Second Edition.) London: Oxford University Press, 1935. By permission.
7. Ezekiel 22:30. (K.J.V.)
8. Ezekiel 22:27. (K.J.V.)
9. Ezekiel 22:26.
10. Ezekiel 22:29.
11. Ezekiel 22:28.
12. Ezekiel 22:30.
13. Victor Hugo.
14. Mark 7:20.
15. 2 Kings 13:14.
16. John 13:34.
17. Matthew 28:19.
18. Mark 8:34.
19. 1 John 1:9.
20. 2 Kings 13:17.
21. From "Faith of Our Fathers," by Frederick W. Faber (1849).
22. Jeremiah 31:15.
23. Jeremiah 32:15.
24. Colossians 1:13.
25. John 16:22.
26. Psalm 24:1. (K.J.V.)
27. Archibald Rutledge, *Life's Extras,* p. 16. Westwood, N.J.: Fleming H. Revell Company, 1928. Used by permission.

CHAPTER X

ON EARTH AS IT IS IN HEAVEN

1. Richard Rothe, from *A Diary of Readings,* edited by John Baillie, Day 85. New York: Charles Scribner's Sons, 1955. (*Still Hours,* English translation 1886, pp. 253-255.) Used by permission.

2. Matthew 6:10.
3. Matthew 5:39. (K.J.V.)
4. Jonah 4:10-11.
5. John Donne (1573-1631), Dean of St. Paul's, *Devotions Upon Emergent Occasions,* XVII. (Spelling modernized.)
6. Luke 10:29.
7. See Matthew 18:21.
8. Luke 10:30.
9. Luke 10:36-37.
10. Genesis 4:9.
11. Genesis 4:10.
12. Matthew 5:46.
13. Walt Whitman.
14. Isaiah 1:17.
15. Hebrews 1:1-2.
16. 1 John 4:19.
17. Romans 12:1.
18. Romans 12:10.
19. William Shakespeare, *The Merchant of Venice,* Act IV, Scene 1, line 199.
20. Luke 10:25.
21. Matthew 25:35-36.
22. William Wordsworth, "Lines Composed a Few Miles Above Tintern Abbey, July 13, 1798."
23. See Luke 10:36.

Chapter XI

CHRIST'S THREE GREATEST COMMANDS

1. Old Gaelic saying.
2. Matthew 13:24; Mark 4:27.
3. Matthew 13:38.
4. Matthew 13:39.
5. Matthew 28:19.
6. Edward Fitzgerald, *The Rubáiyát of Omar Khayyám,* Stanza XCIX.
7. Matthew 13:30,29.
8. Matthew 13:41,43.
9. George Buttrick, *Christ and Man's Dilemma,* p. 180. New York: Abingdon-Cokesbury Press, 1946.
10. John 3:16.
11. Acts 1:8.
12. Matthew 28:19.
13. Luke 24:48.
14. Matthew 5:14.
15. Acts 4:20; 2:32. (K.J.V.)
16. Revelation 2:2ff.
17. Revelation 2:4. (K.J.V.)
18. John 13:34.
19. John 13:35.
20. See Elton Trueblood, *Your Other Vocation.* New York: Harper & Brothers, 1952.
21. See John 18:15ff.
22. Halford Luccock, *Marching Off the Map.* See p. 169. New York: Harper & Brothers, 1952. By permission.

23. John 18:17.
24. Luke 22:27.
25. Luke 22:27.
26. Luke 22:27.
27. John 13:13-15.
28. John 13:16.
29. Matthew 23:11.
30. Matthew 20:28.
31. Mark 8:37.
32. Luke 12:20.
33. Charles Dickens, *A Christmas Carol,* Stave I, "Marley's Ghost."
34. Mark 16:15 (K.J.V.); Acts 1:8; Matthew 23:11.

Chapter XII

UNDER THE EYE OF ETERNITY

1. Alfred, Lord Tennyson, *In Memoriam,* CXXXI, last stanza.
2. Matthew 25:1,14.
3. Matthew 25:19.
4. See *Life* Magazine, November 12, 1956, issue.
5. Matthew 25:40.
6. Matthew 25:23.
7. Matthew 25:23.
8. Matthew 26.
9. Matthew 26:7.
10. Matthew 26:8.
11. Matthew 26:10.
12. See *The Interpreter's Bible,* Volume VII, *Matthew,* p. 570. Nashville: Abingdon Press, 1951.
13. Matthew 26:13.
14. John 3:16.
15. William Shakespeare, *Othello,* Act V, Scene 2.
16. 2 Corinthians 9:6.
17. Matthew 7:2.
18. 2 Corinthians 9:8.
19. 2 Kings 4.
20. Matthew 7:11.
21. Matthew 6:28 and 26.
22. 2 Corinthians 9:8.
23. Luke 12:20.

A WORD AFTER

1. Joshua 3:4.
2. Joshua 3:5.
3. Numbers 10:35. (K.J.V.)